The Munich Air Disaster

The Munich
Air Disaster

Stephen R. Morrin

Gill & Macmillan

Gill & Macmillan Ltd
Hume Avenue, Park West, Dublin 12
with associated companies throughout the world
www.gillmacmillan.ie

© Stephen R. Morrin 2007
978 07171 4110 4

Index compiled by Cover to Cover
Typography design by Make Communication
Print origination by TypeIT, Dublin
Printed by ColourBooks Ltd, Dublin

This book is typeset in 11/13.5 Linotype Minion
and Neue Helvetica.

The paper used in this book comes from the wood pulp of
managed forests. For every tree felled, at least one tree is
planted, thereby renewing natural resources.

A CIP catalogue record for this book is available
from the British Library.

The author and publishers have made every effort to trace all
copyright holders, but if any has been inadvertently overlooked,
we will be pleased to make the necessary arrangement at the
first opportunity.

5 4 3 2 1

Dedicated to my father
who got me started in all this aviation business

'They say that they were the best team we have ever seen. Well, maybe. They say that they may have gone on to be the best team we have ever seen. Well, maybe. But there is one thing for certain. They were the best loved team there has ever been.'

HARRY GREGG

Contents

Author's Note and Acknowledgments

Not everyone who helped me in the research for this book wished to be identified, particularly past and present employees of Manchester United Football Club. They, of course, know who they are and I gratefully acknowledge their invaluable assistance.

I would like to extend my thanks to Sebuda J. Thain, for entrusting me with the responsibility of telling her father's rather complex story and providing me with photographs from the Thain family archive. Thanks also go to Harry Gregg for taking the time to read the manuscript and giving me his critical assessment, helpful comments and invaluable advice.

Among the many books consulted for factual background I must particularly mention the following: *Roger Byrne: Captain of the Busby Babes*, by Iain McCartney; *Viollet: The life of a legendary goalscorer*, by Roy Cavanagh and Brian Hughes; *Harry's Game*, by Harry Gregg; *Manchester United and Beyond*, by Bill Foulkes; *Munich*, by Stanley Williamson; and *Air Disasters*, by Stanley Stewart.

Finally, a special thank you to Fergal Tobin, the Publishing Director at Gill & Macmillan, who saw the potential of this book from the very beginning and gave me the chance to make it a reality.

Stephen R. Morrin
Stockport 2007

Introduction

On 6 February 1958 one of the greatest tragedies ever to strike the world of sport occurred when eight Manchester United footballers were among the twenty-three passengers and crew killed in an air disaster in West Germany. The team were returning in triumph from a European Cup tie against Red Star Belgrade when their Elizabethan airliner crashed in atrocious weather whilst attempting to take off for the third time from Munich-Riem Airport, on the last leg of their journey home. What followed were some of the blackest moments in British footballing history. Among the dead were England first-team regulars Roger Byrne, Duncan Edwards and Tommy Taylor. The United manager Matt Busby, after whom the team had been popularly known as the 'Busby Babes', also came close to perishing with them. No single sporting tragedy since has been more keenly felt. It was an event that was etched in the memory of a generation.

When Matt Busby arrived at Old Trafford just after the war he created his first great team, winning the FA Cup in 1948 and the League Championship in 1952. By the mid fifties Busby's decision to back youth created a second sensational team that took the football world by storm. He had created in just a few short years perhaps the most talented group of players ever seen at one club, destined to dominate football for many years to come. Having conquered the English League with successive titles in 1956 and 1957, they were riding on the crest of a wave and looked set to take Europe by storm. There can be no doubt that Busby's Babes, with an average age of twenty-two, were the cream of the crop, the greatest United side ever assembled, and probably the greatest club side in the history of English football, if not the world. They were still on the threshold of achieving their full potential before fate brutally struck them down.

This book is not just a single narrow narrative about Manchester United and the 'Busby Babes'; it goes much deeper than that. It is also the story of the aircraft's commander, Captain James Thain, who was cruelly set up by the German authorities to take the blame for the tragedy that saw him dismissed by his airline and deprived of his livelihood. Even his own government, not wanting to sour relations with Germany, suppressed evidence that they knew would have cleared his name.

The disaster also irrevocably altered the lives of the bereaved families and surviving players, some of whom were shamefully treated by the most famous and richest club in the world. No story about Munich would be complete without its telling.

Much has been written about Munich and the Busby Babes over the last fifty years. Hardly a year has passed that hasn't seen a newspaper or magazine article giving some new slant on the story and new books and documentaries abound. All of these have had their limitations, which over the years have perpetuated myths, half-truths, exaggeration and distortion of the facts. In the story that follows I hope to give, for the first time, on this fiftieth anniversary, a clear and definitive account of the events before, during and in the aftermath of the disaster. As survivor Harry Gregg says, 'We owe it to the memory of those left behind on that runway to tell it as it was.'

Chapter 1
In the Beginning

It all began on 19 February 1945, when the board of Manchester United appointed Matt Busby as the club's new manager, a position that had been vacant for seven years. Although no one could have known it at the time, his signing was a momentous event in the history of the club, heralding the beginning of a new era of unprecedented success, that would in time make United one of the most famous and best-loved clubs in the world.

Matthew Busby, the son of Helen and Alexander Busby, was born in a lowly two-roomed pitman's cottage in the close-knit mining community of Orbiston, North Lanarkshire in 1909, and raised as a practising Roman Catholic. For Matt, the eldest of four children, it was an impoverished upbringing and at the age of six he suffered the traumatic loss of his father and all his uncles in the First World War. He was destined, like most of his friends in that poor mining village, to work down the pit, and briefly blackened his hands on the coalface before he escaped south, via his ability to play football well.

Ironically, Busby began his footballing career as a seventeen-year-old with Manchester United's neighbours and arch rivals Manchester City, where he was remembered as a stylish and attractive half-back. He played more than two hundred games for the Blues, winning an FA Cup winner's medal in 1934 before being transferred to Liverpool for a fee of £8,000 in 1936. But like many of his contemporaries of that era his playing career was cut short by the outbreak of the Second World War, during which he served in the 9th Battalion of the King's Liverpool Regiment, and later in the Army Physical Training Corps.

When peace was declared in 1945 Busby was still serving in the army as a physical education instructor at Sandhurst, and was officially still a player on Liverpool's books when he received a letter from Louis Rocca, the Manchester United scout, offering him the managerial vacancy at Old Trafford. It wasn't the only offer Busby received at that time — Spurs, Reading and Ayr United all wanted his services — but he turned them all down in favour of the United job. Busby said: 'I got this opportunity to go as manager of Manchester United. I had a soft spot for Manchester after my City days and it attracted me.' His own club, Liverpool, who offered him a coaching job at Anfield, could have quite easily said no to the move, but realising that it was a golden opportunity for Busby they sportingly agreed to release him.

The Manchester United board initially offered him a three-year contract but Busby argued with the directors that it should be extended to at least five years, as this was the time he needed to build a team that would be a major force in English football. The board reluctantly agreed to his wish, and the rest, as we know, is history, with Busby becoming one of the most successful and longest-serving club managers of all time; and the man responsible for the metamorphosis of a club of under-achievers into European Champions. In his twenty-five years with United he created three great teams, winning five League Championships, the FA Cup twice (from four finals), the FA Youth Cup six times (five in succession) and, in 1968, his crowning glory and personal Holy Grail — the European Cup.

It is often assumed that the revival and success of Manchester United was down to Busby and Busby alone. But in fact, as he himself would later admit, it was Manchester businessman James Gibson who saved the club from bankruptcy and oblivion — without him there would have been no Manchester United for Busby to take over.

Gibson, who made his fortune manufacturing army uniforms and in refrigeration storage, came to United's rescue just before Christmas 1931. At the time United were in desperate financial trouble and languishing at the bottom of Division Two. With poor results on the field there was much discontent on the terraces with just 3,500 diehard supporters turning up to watch the opening game of the season. Their luckless manager Herbert Bamlett, a former referee, was sacked in April 1931, leaving the club secretary Walter Crickmer and chief scout Louis Rocca to take over the running of the ailing club, but it seemed a hopeless task to save United from extinction. So dire was the financial situation at this time that club officials had to seriously consider if there were sufficient funds available in the kitty for the team to travel to away games.

The crisis came to a head in Christmas week, when on 18 December the bank refused the club any more credit. With debts of over £17,000 they couldn't even pay the players' wages and were on the brink of bankruptcy and dissolution. James Gibson, a sports fan who loved football, learned of their plight and summoned Walter Crickmer to his home in Hale Barnes, over the border in affluent Cheshire, for a meeting. The meeting was short and to the point. Gibson offered Crickmer a lifeline: a cheque for £2,000 to pay the players' wages and, more importantly, a pledge to act as guarantor for the club's future liabilities. In return for his generosity Gibson asked to be elected chairman and president, a position he would keep for the next twenty years, and he immediately set about transforming the floundering and underachieving club.

Gibson appointed Scott Duncan, a former player with Glasgow Rangers and Newcastle United, as manager on a salary of £8,000 a year. Although Duncan introduced new players into the team United continued to struggle, narrowly avoiding relegation to the Third Division by the narrowest of margins in the 1933–34 season. Meanwhile, their neighbours and rivals Manchester City were going though a successful period, winning the FA Cup in 1934 — with Matt Busby in the team — and had the greater support in Manchester. Gibson, in his efforts to make the club financially sound, was determined to reverse this trend, and amongst other things in an effort to tempt the crowds back he arranged for trains to stop at Old Trafford station so that fans no longer had to walk for miles on match days.

The following season United hauled themselves back from the brink and finished a credible fifth in the Second Division. In the 1935–36 season they were on the up and after a nineteen-match unbeaten run towards the end of the season they won the Second Division title with a 3–2 victory at Bury, where 30,000 fans invaded the pitch to celebrate their return to the top flight of Division One. But it was not to last; relegation and promotion followed over the next two seasons as United tried to find their feet. By this time Scott Duncan had resigned to manage non-league Ipswich Town and Walter Crickmer took over the reins again for another spell as temporary manager.

United ended the 1938–39 season in fourteenth place in the First Division — their highest position in ten years — and with the crowds returning to Old Trafford in ever increasing numbers, injecting much-needed cash into the club's coffers, the future looked bright. But Gibson's plans were soon to be put on hold by darker events beyond his control. The new season had barely got underway when, on Sunday 3 September 1939, Britain declared war on Germany. Two days later the Football League met and cancelled the rest of the season's fixtures and with that league football was suspended for the duration.

When Matt Busby, aged thirty-six and with little experience of management, arrived at Old Trafford to take up his post on 22 October 1945 it was a scene of utter desolation. The ground, on the edge of the vast Trafford Park industrial complex, had received the attention of German bombers on the night of 11 March 1941. The main stand, along with the dressing rooms and offices, lay in ruins; part of the terracing was destroyed and the pitch was badly scorched and unplayable. Now, as Busby surveyed the scene, weeds flourished on the terraces of what was described when it opened in 1910 as one of the finest grounds in the country. Busby may not have had a ground but he had a dream — a dream that would soon transform the image of English football and make Manchester United the greatest football club in the world.

Busby was under no illusions when he accepted the manager's job about the enormity of the task that lay ahead. He was well aware of the hash reality that failure to bring the club success in the short term would ultimately lead to his dismissal, and to survive he knew he would have to be ruthless when necessary. But for the most part he preferred to show the softer side of his personality, leaving some of the more unpopular decisions to others. That underlying streak of ruthlessness would emerge many years later in the aftermath of Munich as he strived to rebuild the club and restore it to its former glory.

With Busby at the helm Manchester United began the long haul back to recovery. They were awarded £322,278 by the War Damage Commission to clear the rubble and rebuild the stadium, but it would be another four years before the work was completed and United could return home. In the meantime makeshift offices were set up nearby in the chairman's premises; a rock-hard compacted piece of ground at the back of the stand was used for practice matches, while a dilapidated Nissen hut served as changing rooms. The immediate problem facing the club while Old Trafford was being reconstructed was where to play their home fixtures. Their neighbours Manchester City came to the rescue, offering the use of their Maine Road ground. Although it seemed like an act of kindness on City's part they did United no favours, charging them £5,000 a year for the hire of the stadium and demanding ten per cent of the gate receipts.

The first signing Busby made as manager was not a player, but the appointment of Jimmy Murphy as chief coach. Busby knew Jimmy as an old friend and opponent on the football field and admired his enthusiasm and passion for the game. Born in the Rhondda Valley, Murphy — the Welshman with an Irish name — loved football from an early age and with the encouragement of his parents and teachers he was soon playing for Wales as a schoolboy international. He recalled: 'I played for Wales as a schoolboy and they were unforgettable times for me; I was passionate and extremely proud to have been selected. Wales at schoolboy level at that time were really a nonentity, but in the year I played we beat England 3–2 in Cardiff and then drew 2–2 with Scotland at Hampden Park. Those results fired my imagination and brought me to the attention of English League clubs.'

His ambition had always been to play for Cardiff City, but he was spotted by a scout from West Bromwich Albion who approached his parents asking if they could sign him. At the age of fourteen Jimmy packed his bags and headed for the Midlands. Having hardly ever travelled further than his native South Wales he soon became homesick, but he was determined to stick it out and make it as a professional footballer. He eventually forced his way into the first team and from that point on he never looked back. In 1933 he was the youngest player in the Welsh national team, winning twenty-two caps and going on to captain the side. Surprisingly, despite his lengthy career he never once scored a single goal in competitive football. In the end, like Busby, it was the war that prematurely ended his playing days.

The Busby-Murphy partnership came about in Bari, Italy, in the summer of 1945, where Sergeant Jimmy Murphy was running a sporting activities club and giving football coaching lessons to the troops. One blistering hot afternoon Murphy was giving a talk to a group of soldiers on the finer points of football tactics. Standing on the edge of the crowd listening intently was Company Sergeant Major Matt Busby, who, along with everyone else, was left spellbound by the fiery Welshman's passionate and enthralling oratory. Busby said: 'He had us all transfixed. He was wonderful. It was as if he had put everybody in a hypnotic trance. It wasn't a speech; it was more like a rousing sermon. I visualised what good he could do for Manchester United.'

When he had finished and the crowd slowly dispersed, Busby walked over and congratulated Jimmy on his talk. He told him that he was taking up the manager's job at Manchester United when he returned home and asked him if he would join him as his assistant. Murphy leapt at the opportunity and, shaking hands with Matt, the deal was done. It was the beginning of the most successful managerial partnership in the history of English football, that would last for over twenty-five years. Many years later Busby recalled that 'Jimmy Murphy was the first and the best signing I ever made for Manchester United.'

As individuals they were as different as chalk and cheese. The pipe-smoking Busby was quietly spoken, urbane, unfailingly diplomatic and with a persuasive charm, but could be as ruthless as anyone when required. By contrast the chain-smoking, whisky-swigging Murphy, whom Busby once said 'had the voice of a cement mixer', shunned the limelight and was never happier than being out on the training ground coaching the young stars of tomorrow. Like Busby, he was a devout Roman Catholic and attended Mass every morning before going to the ground. But as soon as he had changed into his shabby tracksuit and joined the lads on the training field he would swear like a trooper. He was a down-to-earth, no-nonsense coach and always spoke passionately about football. He never had favourites, he treated each player as an individual, and neither did he have time for big-headed prima donnas — 'You win together and you lose together,' he would tell his players. The only common denominator between Busby and Murphy was their passion for football. They had implicit faith in each other, and as a double act they worked as one for Manchester United.

It has been said that Matt Busby was fortunate when he became manager in that he inherited a side of talented players, which included Johnny Carey, Jack Rowley, Allenby Chilton, Stan Pearson, John Aston, Johnny Morris and goalkeeper Jack Crompton. But, as good as it was, it was an ageing team with most of them having lost their best years to the war. But Busby, like a good Scot, made the best of this and it didn't take him long to work his magic. He was an intelligent and observant player in his day and had an acute appreciation of tactics. He made his players more aware of their own talents and continually switched their positions on the field until he found the most effective combinations. A good example of this is how he turned Allenby Chilton, who had previously been a full-back and wing-half, into one of the best centre-halves in the country.

Another player he successfully transferred to a different position was the genial Irishman Johnny Carey, turning him from a half-decent inside-forward into an outstanding full-back. In fact during his United career Carey played in almost every position, including a game in goal when goalkeeper Jack Crompton was taken ill on the day of the match.

The pipe-smoking, teetotal Carey joined United in 1936 from the Dublin club St James's Gate for the bargain price of £250 and established himself as one of the most versatile players of his generation. He lived only a mile and a half from the ground and travelled to Old Trafford on the top deck of the bus on match days with the supporters — imagine that happening today! When hostilities broke out in 1939 he could have quite easily, as a neutral, quietly sat out the war, but instead he volunteered his services, saying that 'a country that pays me my living is certainly worth fighting for'. He was an influential and respected member of the team that led Busby to appoint him captain. Jimmy Murphy classed him as the greatest full-back of all time; he was cool under pressure, superb in the air and gifted with brilliant positional sense. In his seventeen-year career with United he played 344 League and FA Cup games and had the distinction of playing as an international for both Northern Ireland and the Republic. He retired from the game in 1953 and went into management before returning to Old Trafford as a part-time scout.

One of the biggest and most controversial characters in the side was Jack 'Gunner' Rowley. The nickname 'Gunner' came about because of his wartime service with the South Staffordshire infantry as an anti-tank operator and his participation in the D-Day landings at Normandy. When he returned home the name stuck with the fans because of his lethal and accurate shot on goal. He was an aggressive traditional centre-forward and at his peak he was the most feared striker in the country; skilful both in the air and on the ground. He signed for United in October 1937 from Bournemouth for a modest £3,000, aged seventeen, and went on to make 422 appearances, scoring 208 goals. He was the team's top goal scorer in the first four seasons after the war and, until Dennis Viollet came along a few years later, held United's league-scoring record for a single season in 1951–52 with thirty goals. When one considers that his best years were lost to the war, his record seems even the more remarkable.

Rowley is famed for his fiery and confrontational nature, both on and off the field. He was rarely polite to anyone and the young apprentices at Old Trafford lived in fear of him; even Busby had problems with the volatile and turbulent player. Despite his combative and stubborn nature he was intensely loyal to United and one of the finest centre-forwards ever to grace the Old Trafford turf. He left United in 1955 to join Plymouth as player-manager and later went on to manage Oldham (twice), Ajax Amsterdam, Wrexham and Bradford.

The headstrong Charlie Mitten, who prowled the left wing and was described as 'the greatest outside-left that England never had', was considered one of the most talented players in Busby's post-war side. He was fast, a great crosser of the ball with a ferocious and accurate shot. The fans dubbed him 'the Penalty King', for he never failed to convert; in fact he only missed one penalty in the whole of his career. He was so confident in his ability to score from the spot that he would always tell the goalkeeper where he was going to put the ball and still he couldn't save it.

During the summer of 1950 United fans were shocked to read in their morning papers that Mitten had accepted a lucrative offer to play for the Colombian club Bogotá Santa Fe. They had tempted him with a £5,000 signing-on fee, £100 a week in wages, a flat and a car. At a time when professional footballers earned little more than skilled factory workers, the 29-year-old player with a family to support found the offer too good to refuse. Typically, Mitten had failed to inform Busby, his teammates and even his wife of the transaction. An angry Busby told him when he found out: 'You can't do that! You're not allowed to!'

With Colombia a non-FIFA country, any player based there was ostracised from the footballing community, and Mitten was branded by the press the 'Bogotá Bandit'. He played out the 1950–51 season in Latin America, but with the promised finances not materialising and unable to settle he returned home to a hostile reception and found himself frozen out at Old Trafford. The FA fined him six months' wages and suspended him from playing for the same period. Busby took the opportunity to get his own back on the wayward player for stepping out of line and swiftly moved him on to Fulham at a profit for £22,000, where he spent the twilight of his career. After the failure of his South American adventure he turned down another lucrative offer from Real Madrid in order to keep his family together. He later went into management, first with Mansfield Town and then with Newcastle United.

Another stalwart in the side was Stan Pearson, a cost-nothing local lad from Salford who joined the club in 1936. He made his debut aged seventeen in a 7–1 win against Chesterfield. But just as he established himself in the first team his career was interrupted by the outbreak of hostilities. As a gifted inside-forward he was a consistent and deadly striker who fitted in perfectly with Rowley, creating many of his goals, and together they hunted as a pair in the opposition's goalmouth to devastating effect. After a seventeen-year association with United, he signed for Bury in 1954 and later played for and managed Chester. In later life he could be found running the local post office and newsagent's shop in Prestbury, Cheshire.

Some of the other outstanding players that made up the core of Busby's first great team included Johnny Morris, John Aston, Henry Cockburn and goalkeeper Jack Crompton. In 1946 Busby added to the squad when he made his first outright cash signing with the purchase of Jimmy Delaney from Glasgow Celtic for £4,000. Known as 'Old Brittle Bones' because of his frequent injuries, he was considered by many to be past his best, but he defied all his critics and continued to play professional football until he hung his boots up in 1957. He held the unique distinction of having won three Cup winner's medals in three different countries in three different decades — the Scottish Cup with Celtic in 1937, the FA Cup with United in 1948 and the Irish Cup with Derry City in 1954. He also came close with a fourth in the Republic of Ireland with a runner's-up medal with Cork Athletic in 1956.

He left Old Trafford at the end of 1950 and returned home to his native Scotland. After short spells with Aberdeen and Falkirk, he joined Derry City, and ended his 23-year playing career with Elgin.

He spent the rest of his working life as a labourer in his home village, which was considered the norm for retired professional footballers in those austere times.

Busby hinted at what was to come in the future when he said of his first great team: 'I was lucky in having such players at my disposal when I went to Old Trafford. But I realised that you need more than luck to survive. I wanted to achieve a sound club, and I knew that I would need a lot of good, young players to help me in my plans. I never wanted Manchester United to be second to anybody. Only the best would be good enough. I had to have players who would play for me and for United rather than for themselves, and I usually found what I wanted.'

Busby, unlike a lot of managers of the era, preferred a hands-on style of management. Rather than sit in the office he would don a tracksuit and join Jimmy Murphy and his players on the training field — that way he could demonstrate exactly what he expected of them. In those days it was considered revolutionary. It was this attitude that inspired his players and earned him their respect. His captain Johnny Carey recalled: 'When I joined United, Scott Duncan — with spats and a red rose in his button hole — typified a soccer manager. But here was the new boss playing with his team in training, showing what he wanted and how to do it. He was ahead of his time.'

In Busby's first season, United finished a credible fourth in the table, but the best was yet to come. They kicked off the 1946–47 season in great form with five victories, including a 5–0 win over title contenders Liverpool. United, now attracting crowds of over 40,000, battled hard for the First Division Championship all season, but after a brave campaign Liverpool outlasted them with United finishing as runners-up, just one point behind.

In the following season (1947–48) United again finished second in the Championship, this time losing out to Arsenal, while Jimmy Murphy's second team squad finished Central League Champions. But United were not to be denied in the FA Cup competition. Their route to Wembley was arduous, being the only side to be drawn against First Division opposition in every round. With Old Trafford out of action, their task was made all the harder by having to play all their ties at away grounds. In the opening third round they faced Aston Villa in the rain and mud at Villa Park, where United were shocked to concede a goal after just thirteen seconds without even kicking the ball. It was the worst thing that Villa could have done; United regarded it as effrontery and in response turned on a blistering display of attacking football that saw them leading 5–1 at the interval. But Villa was a class team in those days and had no intention of taking it lying down, and to their credit they stormed back in the second half with three goals, making it 5–4. But the Reds had the last word with Stan Pearson scoring his second, United's sixth and the game's tenth goal.

In the following rounds they beat Busby's old club Liverpool 3–0, Charlton 2–0, Preston 4–1 and Derby County in the semi-final, where Stan Pearson scored a devastating hat-trick in a thrilling 3–1 victory. They now faced the mouth-watering prospect of playing Blackpool in the final at Wembley — the first FA Cup final United had played in for thirty-nine years.

Busby and his team set out on the long arduous coach journey to London on the Friday night — there were no motorways in those days — arriving in the capital in the early hours of Saturday morning to snatch a few hours' sleep and be ready to play that afternoon; hardly the best preparation for such an important game. But United were brimful of confidence that they could bring the trophy home; however, they were under no illusions about the quality of the opposition they faced. At the time Blackpool was one of the top First Division sides in the country and the bookies' favourite to lift the cup. The side boasted some well-respected players like Stan Mortensen, Harry Johnston and 'The Wizard of the Dribble' himself, Stanley Matthews, recognised as being the greatest player of his day. The final lived up to all expectations and is still remembered nostalgically as one of the best ever staged at Wembley. The United team line-up was: Crompton, Carey, Aston, Anderson, Chilton, Cockburn, Delaney, Morris, Rowley, Pearson and Mitten.

Blackpool clearly showed their intentions early on, when after only twelve minutes Stan Mortensen broke free of the United defence and charged towards goal only to be chopped down by

Allenby Chilton, sending him sprawling inside the box. Today the foul would have seen Chilton marching back to the dressing room, but back in 1948 it was considered part of the rough and tumble of the game. The referee controversially pointed towards the penalty spot, even though the initial contact was made a yard outside the area. Eddie Shimwell's poorly taken penalty somehow managed to evade the diving United keeper Jack Crompton to put Blackpool one up.

United managed to level the game in the twentieth-eighth minute with a slice of luck, when Delaney lobbed a speculative ball towards the Blackpool goal; confusion and misunderstanding between Eric Hayward and his goalkeeper Joe Robinson let in Jack Rowley, who had little more to do than walk the ball over the line to equalise. So far it had been an evenly contested game and the stalemate lasted only five minutes, when Stanley Matthews from a free kick found Kelly, whose pass put Mortensen through to fire the ball past a startled Crompton into the back of the net.

After the interval United piled on the pressure and were rewarded when Morris's quickly taken free kick split the Blackpool defence wide open, allowing Rowley's diving header to hit the roof of the net to level the score at 2–2. With ten minutes remaining and the game poised on a knife-edge, Blackpool came close to scoring when Crompton made a brilliant save from a Mortensen piledriver. Within seconds Crompton cleared the ball upfield to find Stan Pearson, whose 25-yard shot flew in off the post, putting United ahead for the first time. Three minutes later United sealed the game when Anderson unleashed a shot that was cruelly deflected off Kelly's head, leaving the Blackpool keeper wrong-footed. All he could do was watch as the ball sailed into the back of the net to give United a memorable 4–2 victory and lift the FA Cup for the first time since 1909.

Unfortunately James Gibson, whose financial backing and belief had carried United so far, suffered a stroke prior to the final and was unable to travel with the team to Wembley. On their way back to Manchester the following day Busby had the team coach diverted to his home in Hale Barnes where he and the triumphant players presented him with the Cup. With no suitable display case at Old Trafford the trophy was wrapped in a blanket and kept in the bottom of a wardrobe in the chairman's spare bedroom.

The FA Cup was Manchester United's first silverware under Busby's management. In just a few austere post-war years he had created by far the best attacking, entertaining and exciting team in the country. Thousands were now turning out each week to watch them at home and away. Their journey to Wembley alone was witnessed by over 300,000 spectators — an aggregate record that still stands today.

In the season following the Cup win, United, for the third time in as many seasons, finished runners-up in the First Division. This was followed by a fourth, then another second place. Then in 1952, as Busby had long predicted, they won the Championship for the first time in forty-one years, four points ahead of Spurs. The only question being asked by the supporters and football pundits was why had it taken them so long? Sadly, the chairman James Gibson didn't live long enough to see the trophy return to Old Trafford; he died in September 1951 after suffering a fatal stroke. The only memorial that exists to this kind benefactor, whose financial commitment saved and sustained the club for twenty years, is a small plaque fixed to the bridge over Old Trafford station, where today it goes unnoticed by a new generation of United fans as they pour out of the trains on match days. If asked, the majority would have no idea who James Gibson was.

No sooner was the Championship title theirs than the team began to slide, losing six of the first eleven games in the opening season. Their fluency and poise seemed to have deserted them overnight and by October they were struggling at the foot of the table. Busby was hardly surprised by this turn of events; he knew the team was growing older and had passed its peak. From that point on he began to implement the plan he had formulated when he first arrived at the club in 1945. He was about to create the greatest Manchester United team of all time that would push back the frontiers of British football and capture the hearts of the nation.

Chapter 2
Birth of the Babes

Remember the fifties? It was the time when Britain slowly emerged from the shadow of war and the grim austerity of the late forties. The country and its people now looked forward to the immediate future with a sense of optimism and expectation that had long been denied them. The coronation of the Queen in 1953 ushered in the beginning of a glorious new 'Elizabethan' age. Hillary and Tenzing had conquered Everest, Watson and Crick had unlocked the structure of DNA, Roger Bannister broke the four-minute mile and Winston Churchill was knighted.

It was a decade when bad manners were not tolerated, people got married first and *then* lived together, and divorce and homosexuality were viewed as shameful. Men slicked back their hair with Brylcreem, would always stand up for a woman on a bus and never swear in front of the opposite sex. It was safe for children to play in the street and they were encouraged to do so. Cigarette-smoking was fashionable, television was a luxury and Teddy boys in their drape coats and crepe-soled shoes lounged around in coffee bars.

It was the decade before supermarkets, frozen food, credit cards, ballpoint pens and the Pill. But it was also a decade of new beginnings. Suddenly rationing was out and rock and roll was in. A new wave of optimism and affluence swept the country, moving

Prime Minister Harold Macmillan to say to the British people, 'You have never had it so good.'

It was also the decade that saw the beginning of a revolution in British football with the emergence of an exciting, young and entertaining football team, the like of which had never been seen before. By the mid fifties they swept all before them and looked set to reign over their rivals, both at home and abroad, for the next decade. With their beguiling skills, youthful exuberance and sportsmanship they captured the imagination of all who saw or read about them. They were the Busby Babes.

Back in 1945 when Matt Busby became manager, the Babes were just a twinkle in his eye. In those days if a club wanted a new player they simply went out and bought one and hoped he would fit in with the rest of the team. Now, after winning the FA Cup in 1948 and the Championship in 1952 with his first great team, Busby aspired to achieve even greater heights by replacing his ageing team with a new, youthful team assembled from scratch.

His shrewd idea was to snap up talented players for little or no outlay when they were young and avoid the massive transfer fees demanded for more established footballers. He began his search in the back streets, looking for lads in his own image who loved football and were hungry for success. Busby said, 'From the very start I had envisaged making my own players, having a kind of nursery so that they could be trained in the kind of pattern I was trying to create for Manchester United.' And so began the legend of the Busby Babes, as one by one star-struck youngsters, with their football kit under their arms, arrived each week at Old Trafford for trials. Hundreds came but only the exceptional few were chosen.

Busby's aim was not just to build a First Division Championship winning side, which any other football manager would be more than happy to achieve; his vision went much deeper than that. He explained, 'I did not set out to build a team: the task ahead was much bigger than that. What I really embarked upon was the building of a system which would produce not one team but four or five, each occupying a rung on the ladder the summit of which was the First xi.'

From the very beginning of his appointment, Busby wanted Manchester United to be more than just a business; he wanted to create a family club, instilling in everyone, from players to management, a sense of belonging and community spirit. This stemmed from his own socialist and religious upbringing in Lanarkshire where family and community were so important. Above all he regarded the welfare of the youngsters that joined the club as paramount. He knew from his own experience the hardships faced by young lads leaving home for the first time and felt a moral obligation for their welfare.

An important aspect of this care was their living arrangements. Those who came from outside Manchester were placed into hand-picked lodgings close to the ground, run by carefully vetted landladies, where they shared rooms and ate around a communal table. Mrs Watson's boarding house at number 5 Birch Avenue was typical of the accommodation provided by the club. Located near the Lancashire County Cricket ground, a stone's throw from Old Trafford, she catered for up to twenty boarders at any one time, including commercial travellers and truck drivers. Duncan Edwards, David Pegg, Tommy Taylor and Bobby Charlton all lived there at one time or another. For the handful of the older players who were married, like Bill Foulkes, Roger Byrne and Geoff Bent, they were allocated club houses located within a two-mile radius of the ground for a peppercorn rent.

In return Busby expected respect, discipline, loyalty and good manners at all times from his young charges. Strict rules at Old Trafford also had to be adhered to, such as wearing a collar and tie, calling the senior players Mister and always knocking on the first-team dressing-room door before entering. Nor would he tolerate bad language, either at the club or when out on their own in public.

In the fifties a promising schoolboy could not sign for a club until he had officially left school, and then only as an amateur receiving no pay. So until he reached the age of seventeen and signed professional forms entitling him to be paid a wage, he was encouraged to continue his education, or take up a trade or profession alongside his playing career as a safeguard in the event that things didn't work out. For example, Duncan Edwards, David Pegg and Geoff Bent became apprentice joiners, Bill Foulkes a collier, whilst Bobby Charlton chose to work in a local engineering company earning £2 a week and training at the club in the evenings. The only other option open to them was to join the United ground staff, which involved undertaking various jobs around Old Trafford such as tending the football pitch, maintaining the stands and terraces, sweeping and mopping the dressing rooms, cleaning boots, running messages and anything else they were called upon to do. In many ways ground duties were the easier option, strolling in as they did at nine-thirty in the morning and knocking off at four-thirty.

As soon as they arrived at Old Trafford they came under the supervision of Jimmy Murphy to be coached, groomed and moulded into the United stars of tomorrow. In the dressing room he would hold up a Manchester United shirt and tell them, 'When you put on this jersey you will feel ten-foot tall and it will make you run through brick walls. Wear it with pride, lads.' Murphy was a wonderful coach with tremendous powers of motivation that inspired incredible devotion from the youngsters. He was a hard taskmaster and set high standards. It was not unusual to see him out on the training ground late into the afternoon with dusk approaching, putting the young players through their paces. He never used a coaching manual; he did it in his own unique way, teaching the fundamentals that were the foundation of the game: attacking, defending, passing and, most important of all, playing as a team. 'Keep it simple . . . pass to a red shirt,' he would urge them.

Assisting and supporting Murphy were first-team trainer Tom Curry and coach Bert Whalley. Bert was burly man with a mop of snow-white hair and always brimming with vitality. He had been a former wing-half with United, making thirty-three appearances before a serious eye injury curtailed his playing career in 1947. Busby decided to keep him on the staff at Old Trafford — an act of kindness Bert never forgot. He was also a Methodist lay preacher — which puts to rest the long-held belief that Manchester United was a Catholic-only club. He was a true gentleman, quiet and softly spoken; a particularly good influence on the youngsters, he truly cared for their welfare. Every Friday without fail he would give each of the players a handwritten letter giving them his opinion on how they had performed that week and what to expect from the opposition they faced in the next game. He also kept them up to date with everything else that was happening at the club. It was things like this that gave the youngsters a feeling that they were part of a family, which in turn generated loyalty and team spirit.

Tom Curry, 'Tosher' to everyone at Old Trafford, was a kind, warm-hearted man and a father figure to the youngsters. Like Whalley, he was deeply religious. He had been a player with Newcastle United when they challenged for the League Championship in 1920 and 1921. In 1929 he left on a free transfer to Stockport County, and a year later became Carlisle United's trainer before joining United in 1934. Like Busby and Murphy a generation later, most of his playing career was lost to a world war. He was a great believer in physical fitness and Matt Busby described him as 'the best trainer in Britain'. Although he mainly worked with the first-team players he would often freely give his time in the youth training sessions, offering help and advice when required. His other role, in accordance with club rules, was the discipline of the youngsters who, for their part, made sure that any hanky-panky they got up to remained as far as possible undetected.

It was assumed by many that the reason United had the monopoly on young talented players was that they had an elaborate army of scouts scouring the country at any one time. This is far from the truth; in fact United had only one full-time scout and that was Joe Armstrong — the man who, it was said, could spot future stars on a foggy day. When he wasn't out scouting he could be found in his other role manning the Old Trafford switchboard. Working with him were half a dozen part-time scouts who regularly patrolled the playing fields of schoolboy fixtures up and down the country on the lookout for the sort of vibrant young talent that Busby and Murphy coveted. There were also three scouts based in Ireland — a rich breeding ground of schoolboy stars in the fifties — Billy Behan, Bob Bishop and Bob Harper. It was Harper who was later to discover a scrawny youngster called George Best playing in the back streets of Belfast.

By the early 1950s Busby's youth policy began to yield startling results, with a stream of exceptionally talented schoolboy prospects arriving at Old Trafford. Jackie Blanchflower, Mark Jones, Dennis Viollet, Bill Foulkes and Geoff Bent were amongst some of the first. They were soon followed by Albert Scanlon, Eddie Colman, Duncan Edwards and Bobby Charlton. Both Busby and Murphy knew it was only a matter of time before these exciting precocious youngsters would be ready to take their place in the first team.

With so many accomplished players now at the club Busby could quite easily have fielded two better-than-average First Division sides. The difficulty he had was where to play these sixteen- and seventeen-year-old talents. The Central League was deemed too harsh, filled as it was in the main by combat-experienced veterans who would take great pleasure in physically tearing the youngsters apart. Then in 1952 the FA Youth Cup came to the rescue. The competition was set up to bridge the gap between players of school-leaving age and senior football. Ninety-three clubs entered in its inaugural season. Besides Manchester United, Wolverhampton Wanderers and other top First Division clubs, the competition attracted some unlikely entrants, such as Huntley Palmers Biscuits, White Rose of York, St Mary's of Dorset and Walthamstow Avenue, to name a few.

It came as no surprise that United, having snapped up all the best youngsters in the country, dominated the competition right from the start, winning the first five finals. There were some notable scorelines along the way including a 23–0 demolition of Nantwich in the first season, a record that still stands today. United's success in the tournament proved beyond any doubt that Busby's youth policy was consistently producing the calibre of player that would eventually progress to the first team, saving the club an enormous amount in transfer fees in the coming years. To prove the point, Bobby Charlton, Duncan Edwards, Albert

Scanlon, Eddie Colman, David Pegg, Kenny Morgans and Liam Whelan, the nucleus of the Babes, all began their careers in the youth team.

The competition gave the youngsters the experience of playing in large stadiums in front of large crowds, giving them that 'big match' atmosphere. It also helped to develop their competitive edge, confidence and team spirit, which greatly eased their transition into first-team football. These youthful cavaliers with their daring, attractive and entertaining style of play attracted large crowds to Old Trafford, where attendances sometimes outstripped that of some First Division games.

As the 1951–52 Championship season came to a close, Busby and Murphy were on the lookout for a powerful centre-forward to take the place of the great Jack Rowley, who was nearing the end of his career. None of the home-grown youngsters seemed to fit the bill in that position, so the United scouts were alerted up and down the country to find the man that could lead the forward line.

It was around this time that United's reserves were playing Barnsley across the Pennines in Yorkshire. Albert Scanlon was selected as reserve and took his place in the dugout with Jimmy Murphy. From the moment the whistle blew the United defence was torn apart by a six-foot tall youngster with black curly hair called Tommy Taylor. He was fast, fearless, gracefully athletic and the best header of a ball that Murphy had ever seen. If that was not enough he had the almost supernatural ability to hang in mid-air while waiting to head the ball into the back of the net.

From the dugout a chain-smoking Murphy screamed at his players for allowing him to score three goals. Albert Scanlon recalls Jimmy mumbling to himself, 'That's him, that's him. He's the one.' Although Murphy was angry to concede three goals to lowly Barnsley, he was secretly excited when the final whistle blew. It was obvious to him that Taylor was the centre-forward they were looking for and he couldn't wait to tell Matt he had found their man.

On hearing Murphy's news, Busby dispatched his scouts to watch Taylor in action at every available opportunity and all the reports that came back confirmed that Tommy was a great prospect. The hunt was now on to sign him, but it was not to be an easy task, beset by problems along the way. It was rumoured that seventeen First Division clubs all wanted to sign Tommy; this was reduced to a handful when the Barnsley directors decided to cash in and demanded a fee of £30,000 — an outrageous sum at the time for a Second Division player.

Jimmy Murphy made several trips across the Pennines to talk to the player about moving to Old Trafford even before Barnsley officially put him up for sale. Tommy was a star at his own club and he really didn't want to leave, and with the maximum wage in force what was the point? But Barnsley was not a rich club and in order to balance the books they had no alternative but to put him up for sale to the highest bidder. Cardiff, another club anxious to sign him, upped the price to £35,000 and the Barnsley directors were ready to do the deal when Tommy stepped in and said, 'I'm joining one club only and that is Manchester United.'

On the day the transfer was finalised, Tommy was at the cinema enjoying a film, when suddenly a message flashed up on the screen: 'Tommy Taylor, please report to Oakwell immediately'. He arrived to find a smiling Matt Busby with pen in hand waiting for his signature. Although the agreed transfer fee was a record £30,000, Busby didn't want to burden the youngster with the pressure of a price tag of that magnitude so the official fee was £29,999. It is said that Busby gave the odd pound to Lily Wilby, the Barnsley tea lady who had made endless cups of tea during the long-drawn-out transfer negotiations. All that Tommy received under the rules was £10! The signing was big news in Barnsley; Tommy leaving home was even on TV. So in the end Busby got his man and Lily treated herself to a new hairdo!

Busby said of Taylor: 'Tommy was the player we needed to round the team off, to complete the picture — a big strong finisher. He was brilliant in the air, so good that he would rank with the greats. Not only could he head for goal with great power, he could also turn in the air and head delicately to a man either behind him or alongside. He was also a great finisher with his feet, and an unselfish player. He wanted to score goals himself, naturally, everyone does, but he really didn't mind who scored them as long as the ball went in. He was just as happy making goals as scoring them himself.'

When Tommy arrived at Old Trafford he was regarded as the final piece of the United jigsaw. Such was the wealth of talent now at the club, Taylor was the only player brought in from outside in four years. He made his debut against Tom Finney's Preston North End in March 1953 at Old Trafford, scoring twice, once with a header from outside the penalty area. With his perpetual smile and lethal goal-scoring ability he was quickly dubbed by the press and supporters 'The Smiling Executioner'.

Bill Foulkes, in his autobiography *Manchester United and Beyond*, recalls an incident that was typical Tommy:

> One of my most hair-raising memories of Tommy takes me back to a celebration at the Midland Hotel, in the centre of Manchester, after one of our European wins. At the end of the evening Teresa and I were hailing a taxi when Tommy, who lived not far from us in Sale, grinned: 'You don't have to bother with that, I'll give you a lift.' I wasn't too sure because he could be a bit cavalier, to say the least, but Teresa thought it would be fun, so we went. True to character, Tommy put his foot down and soon we were approaching the roundabout at Trafford Bar pretty fast. As he attempted to negotiate the turn, he lost control, the car spun like a top and I thought: 'This is the end.' Miraculously, though, we didn't hit anything and we jumped out, relieved to be alive. Then, on asking a few pertinent questions, we discovered that he had no brakes, that it wasn't his car — he had borrowed it from a chum — and that he had no driving licence! On closer inspection, we saw that the car was a dilapidated old thing, so we declined his gleeful invitation to continue the journey and hailed a taxi.

Another Yorkshire player to arrive at the Old Trafford nursery was David Pegg from Doncaster. A schoolboy prodigy, he played for Yorkshire Boys and was capped five times for England Schoolboys before being snapped up by United straight from school. At first he played mainly in the reserves, but after being promoted to the first team in the 1955–56 season he became a regular in the side. Like his teammate Dennis Viollet he was an elegant mover and appeared to glide over the football field like a hovercraft. In his day he was one of the most talented wingers in the Football League. Even Real Madrid had a healthy respect for the player, going so far as to sign a new defender specifically to combat his talents in a European Cup game.

With his film-star looks, flashing smile and a hairstyle to match, he attracted a host of female admirers on and off the football field. He also had an army of hero-worshipping male fans who aspired to be like him. These dedicated followers of fashion copied Pegg's style of dress in every detail and even sported the same hairdo. There was a shop in the Collyhurst district of Manchester called Harry the Barbers that had photographs of all the Busby Babes pinned up on the wall. It was here that young lads would come in on a Saturday morning and, forgoing their usual short back and sides, would glance at the portraits on the wall, sit in the chair and ask Harry for a David Pegg cut.

Making up a trio of Yorkshire players, alongside Tommy Taylor and David Pegg, was the giant defender Mark Jones. Captain of Barnsley Schoolboys, he gave up his job as a bricklayer's apprentice for the chance to join United in 1948. As understudy to his boyhood hero Allenby Chilton, his senior chances were limited in his early years at the club, and when he was promoted to the first team in 1954 he had a continual battle with Jackie Blanchflower for the centre-half position. Tall and powerfully built, he was fearless in the tackle and regarded as one of the hardest headers of the ball in the English League. Just before the disaster he had regained his position in the side and was playing some of the best football of his career.

The way the United scouting system worked was simple and straightforward: Joe Armstrong would pass on the information gleaned from the scouts to Jimmy Murphy and Bert Whalley who would then go on and watch the player several times to assess their ability. If they came up to expectations the next stage was to meet the parents. It was through this system that Duncan Edwards, Bobby Charlton, David Pegg, Albert Scanlon and Eddie Colman, to name a few, were discovered.

A typical example of the efficiency of the United recruitment process was how they captured the schoolboy star Dennis Viollet from under the noses of their rivals Manchester City. Dennis lived within a corner kick of Maine Road and his parents, being staunch City supporters, wanted nothing more than to see their talented son wear the sky-blue shirt, rather than the red of United.

The story begins during the war years. Dennis, who was about nine at the time, was playing football in the street with some of his friends when a soldier on leave joined in. That soldier, it was discovered years later, was none other than Matt Busby. He was so taken by the footballing skills of one so young that he made a note of his name for future reference before going on his way.

A few years later Dennis had come on by leaps and bounds and was now captaining Manchester Schoolboys as well as playing regularly for his country. Frank Swift, the legendary City and England goalkeeper, greatly admired the young Dennis and tipped off the Manchester City management that he was an exceptional prospect and should be seen as soon as possible. Some time later Frank, who lived nearby, bumped into Dennis's father in the street and asked him if City had been in touch yet about his son. 'No, not a word,' he told him. Frank was dismayed by the club's laxity and said that he would personally arrange a meeting for him and Dennis to meet the chief scout at Maine Road.

A few days later Dennis and his father duly made their way to the Maine Road offices at the appointed time and were told by the girl in reception to sit down and wait until called. Over an hour passed with no sign of being seen. Annoyed and irritated, Mr Viollet, who was due back at work, knocked on the office door and asked why they weren't being attended to, only to be glibly told that the scout had gone out on an appointment, having left without giving them any explanation or apology for his absence. Mr Viollet lost his temper and vented his anger on the poor girl before storming out of the office with the young Dennis in tow.

The following day there was a knock on the door. Dennis

opened it to see a smiling Matt Busby standing on the doorstep, asking to see his parents. He had remembered the nine-year-old playing in the street years earlier and had been following his progress closely ever since. Within a few hours Busby, using persuasive charm, made a powerful case that Manchester United was the only club for their son.

Two years later Viollet graduated from Busby's nursery, making his debut in a 2–1 win against Newcastle United at St James' Park in April 1953, taking over from the legendary Stan Pearson. Physically, Viollet did not give the appearance of a professional footballer. He was pale-faced and painfully thin to the point of looking undernourished. He looked pathetically ill-equipped to endure ninety minutes of the rough and tumble of a top First Division game.

But one thing Dennis had was style. Everything about his play was silky smooth. On the football field he didn't run, he glided like quicksilver. He had searing acceleration, inch-perfect passing and was blessed with instinctive ball control. As a goal poacher he was second to none, always lurking ghost-like in space waiting to snatch half-chances. In his thirteen-year career with United he scored a phenomenal seven hat-tricks, and to this day he still holds United's goal-scoring record for a single season with thirty-two goals. Not even Law, Best or Cantona came close to equalling that record and it is unlikely to be bettered.

Dennis loved to take his mum to United games, where he would introduce her to the players before she took her place in the stand with the rest of the supporters, shouting encouragement to her son. In their book *Viollet: the Life of a Legendary Goalscorer*, Roy Cavanagh and Brian Hughes relate a humorous incident involving Dennis's mother at one match:

At Old Trafford in the early 1960s, a well-known wag — the one who used to take a pet monkey on his shoulder to United games — was heckling Dennis something terrible. He was not having one of his better games. 'Aye, eye,' the wag bellowed, 'What's up, Viollet? Too much night clubbing again, 'ave yer?' Suddenly, he felt a couple of short, hard raps on his shoulder. He turned round to see a very angry woman wielding an umbrella. 'Don't you dare insult my son like that!' shouted a red-faced Mrs Viollet, clearly a feisty lady when occasion demanded!

Off the football field Dennis certainly liked to live it up. Always immaculately dressed, he was regularly spotted in the nightclubs of downtown Manchester, especially the Continental, Deno's and the Cromford, where he liked to relax with a drink. From all the stories there was no doubt he was an out-and-out ladies' man, a real charmer, and he was rarely seen in public without a crowd of nubile young women in his company. Even his marriage at an early age didn't seem to curb his night-time excursions. A joke doing the rounds at the time said that the Manchester Courts printed their paternity forms with his name already on! In many ways he was the forerunner of George Best, although his friends and team-mates stressed that he never had a drink problem.

Towards the end of that somewhat shaky 1952–53 season some of the youngsters, such as David Pegg, Duncan Edwards, Bill Foulkes, Jackie Blanchflower and Dennis Viollet were drafted in by Busby for the occasional game in the first team, pushing out some of the post-war veterans. But United couldn't achieve the heights of the previous season and finished a modest eighth in the League.

Eddie Colman, the 'cheeky chappie' from Salford, was typical of the talented youngsters that arrived at Old Trafford in the early fifties. He was brought up by his parents, Dick and Liz, in a two-up two-down terraced house on Archie Street in the Ordsall district — the fictional setting for the TV soap *Coronation Street*. Like other post-war kids he began playing football around the cobbled streets and levelled bomb sites near his home before progressing to the school team. Eddie certainly had talent and before long he was playing for Salford Boys, where he was spotted by United. Joining the club as an amateur in 1952, he quickly moved up through the junior teams and into the Youth Cup side. Just before his nineteenth birthday in November 1955, he made his debut against Bolton Wanderers at Burnden Park, making an indelible impression on the game, after which he was an ever-present member of the first team.

At 5 feet 7 inches and under 10 stone he was the smallest player in the team, but what he lacked in physique he more than compensated for with the ball-winning skills and astute accurate passing that made him a big hit with the Old Trafford fans. The press soon dubbed him 'Snake Hips' after his defence-splitting deceptive body swerve that sent his opponents reeling the wrong way. Harry Gregg once said that when Eddie swayed the girders on the grandstand swayed with him.

Eddie was the extrovert in the team with a great sense of humour, always smiling and the first one to jump up at a party and burst into song. Wherever Eddie was there was fun. He was a big fan of Louis Armstrong and Frank Sinatra; he collected all their records and was a familiar sight hanging around Barry Kelsall's music shop near the cathedral in the city centre with half a dozen of his teammates. Eddie was the trendy one amongst the Babes, with long sideburns and never without a comb to tidy his hair. He was one of the first players to wear drainpipe trousers and 'winkle-picker' shoes. For all his fame as a Busby Babe he never made anything of it. When out on the town and girls asked him what he did for a living, he would tell them that he worked in Trafford Park, or that he was a docker, but his favourite line was, 'I'm a painter and decorator.'

Marjorie English, Eddie's girlfriend at the time, remembers how on Saturday evenings after a match they would all gather around the piano in the Bridge pub in Sale, a few miles from the ground, for a pint and a sing-song. It was there that Eddie, who really fancied himself as a crooner, would belt out his favourite song — 'Pennies from Heaven'. But the player with the best voice, according to Marjorie, was none other than Bobby Charlton.

The 1953–54 season was one of major changes at Old Trafford. The legendary Johnny Carey retired to become manager of Blackburn Rovers, Stan Pearson was transferred a few miles up the road to Bury and Jack Rowley went south to Plymouth Argyle. On the field of play United got off to a poor start and by October were languishing at the foot of the table. Although disappointed by their inconsistent form, Busby was not unduly worried. With a wealth of young talent waiting in the wings ready to give the team new impetus, he was about ready to make a decisive move and promote a clutch of his fledglings into the first team. It would prove to be a defining moment.

Busby recalled: 'We played a friendly at Kilmarnock and I played half a dozen of the youngsters. They did well and we won 3–0. Then as I walked the golf course in the next few days, I pondered whether this was the time to play them all in the League team. One or two had already come into the side, and I decided that I would go the whole way with the youngsters.'

In the next league match against Huddersfield, Busby fielded a team that included Roger Byrne, Duncan Edwards, Dennis Viollet, Tommy Taylor, Bill Foulkes, Jackie Blanchflower, with Ray Wood in goal. Although they only came away with a draw they gave a good account of themselves. Busby decided to keep faith with the youngsters and was repaid with a 6–1 thrashing of Cardiff at Ninian Park, and a week later at Old Trafford they dispatched Blackpool 4–1 with a hat-trick from Tommy Taylor. The new-look youthful team was beginning to gel at the highest level, but they didn't find overnight success, managing to finish the season in fourth place. But there was no doubt in Busby's mind that his Babes were on their way to greater things.

The origin of the name 'The Busby Babes' came from the pen, or more correctly the typewriter of Tom Jackson — the sports writer who covered United for the *Manchester Evening News* and another victim of Munich. He first used the name in a match report on 24 November 1951 when Busby introduced youngsters Roger Byrne and Jackie Blanchflower into the first team in a game against Liverpool at Anfield. From that day on the name was universally adopted by everyone and became part of United folklore. Although Busby despised the title he had given his name to — he preferred 'The Red Devils' — he eventually learned to live with it.

Roger Byrne holds the distinction of being the first of the Babes, arriving at Old Trafford in 1948 and making his debut in November 1951. Born in the Manchester suburb of Gorton in 1929,

he earned a scholarship to Burnage Grammar School where he
excelled at sport, earning a place in the Burnage Old Boys football
team. During his two-year spell of National Service with the RAF
he played rugby, boxed for his unit and was a fine gymnast, but
surprisingly he was not considered good enough to play for the
services football team.

It was while playing for his local club, Ryder Brow, that he came
to the attention of the United scout Joe Armstrong and was offered
amateur terms with the club. Within a few months he signed
professional forms and soon made his breakthrough into the first
team. He was an intelligent, self-confident player, rock solid in
defence, brilliant at intercepting passes and one of the fastest full-
backs in the country. But for all his skill — according to Bill
Foulkes — he couldn't head a ball to save his life.

Roger could be a stubborn and hot-headed individual and was
never afraid to voice his opinion, even at times defying Busby. One
confrontation with the boss came during an end-of-season tour of
the United States in 1952 and nearly resulted in him being sent
home. United were playing a so-called friendly against the Atlas
Club of Mexico in Los Angeles. It was a bad-tempered match and
the Mexicans, having no regard for the rules of the game, gave the
United players a good kicking at every opportunity. Roger, after
being kicked into the air by one Mexican player, thumped the next
one who came near him. Needless to say the referee gave him his
marching orders. Busby, in his book *Soccer at the Top*, recalled the
incident:

Atlas were a rough, tough lot. Seeing how things were going, I
told Johnny Carey to instruct the team to keep their heads, keep
together and keep calm. This he did, but Roger defied him and
was sent off.

I was annoyed about this. I did not like Manchester United
players being sent off, though I know before anybody jumps
that we have had our share of these unhappy occurrences. I
especially did not like my players to be sent off abroad, where
the club and national reputations suffer more than an
individual player's reputation. Nor did I like my instructions to

be forgotten, even allowing for provocation, of which there was plenty.

So I had to make my point once more. I was the boss. We would do it my way. I told Roger that he must apologise to Johnny Carey or I would send him home the next day. I would give him two hours to do it in. No more than fifteen minutes later Johnny Carey came to see me to say: 'Roger has been to apologise.'

So Roger rose in my estimation, high in it though he already was. I knew it was only a lapse into a headstrong state that had caused his dismissal. Now he had shown that he was big enough to apologise.

When Allenby Chilton retired in 1954, Busby lost a dependable and commanding captain and he had no hesitation in appointing Roger as his successor. By this time he had matured and commanded great respect of his fellow players and led by example. During his three years as captain he was held in great affection by all who knew him and saw him play; truly one of Manchester United's all-time greats.

Roger boosted his meagre earnings writing a weekly football column in the *Manchester Evening News*. With that and his win bonuses, of which there were many, he was able to splash out on a black Morris Minor — his pride and joy — making him one of the first of the Babes on four wheels. Even though there was little in the way of traffic on the roads in those days, Busby always cautioned his players to be careful as even a minor bump could deprive him of a player for weeks. His fears were soon to be realised.

One freezing day in January 1952 Roger was driving down an icy Wilbraham Road on his way to Old Trafford for training. Suddenly without warning a delivery van turned into his path, forcing him to swerve to avoid a collision. Skidding across the road, the car smashed through the garden wall of Matt Busby's next-door neighbour, ending up in the front garden. On hearing the crash Busby jumped up from the breakfast table and rushed out and was taken aback when he discovered the identity of the unfortunate driver. Recovering from his initial shock, he helped his shaken but uninjured captain from his wrecked car and drove him on to the ground where inevitably there was some merciless leg-pulling for the rest of the day from his teammates.

At the time of his death at Munich, Byrne was just two days short of his twenty-ninth birthday — somewhat old to be called a Babe. But if somehow the disaster had been avoided he would probably — after winning thirty-three successive caps — have captained England in the 1958 World Cup finals playing alongside teammates Tommy Taylor and Duncan Edwards. He was also widely tipped as the man most likely to succeed Matt Busby as manager.

Albert Scanlon was another street-educated player recruited locally. As a former Manchester Schoolboy star he joined United as an amateur in 1950 and made his first-team debut in 1954. He was a player of great potential, a fast orthodox winger with a deadly left foot that scored some unforgettable goals. At the time of Munich he had just edged David Pegg out of the team and his future looked bright.

He was one of the great characters in the side and his fellow Babes nicknamed him Joe Friday, after the detective played by Jack Webb in the American police drama *Dragnet*, shown on British TV at the time. Like his fictional alter ego Scanlon had a preference for wearing the same style white raincoat. When he arrived at any foreign destination on his travels with United — even though he had never been there before — he would amaze his teammates with the countless number of local contacts he seemed to know. It was Harry Gregg who eventually discovered his secret. It turned out that as soon as Albert arrived at the hotel where they were staying, he would thumb through the local telephone directory until he came across an English-sounding name. The chances were they were expats, so he would give them a call, meet up, have a few drinks and get a free guided tour with no need to learn the lingo.

One player who was taken for granted by the fans and the sporting press was Bill Foulkes. He joined United in March 1950 from St Helens Boys' Club and combined playing with working as a miner at Lea Green Colliery. He was not regarded as one of the most skilful players in the side and Foulkes himself didn't think he was good enough to make the grade as a professional footballer. It was only after being called up to play for England — just hours after surfacing from a shift down the pit — that convinced him to give up his job at the colliery. He made his first-team appearance halfway through the 1952–53 season as right-back, before moving to his favoured position of centre-half. Bill was big, tough and dependable but above all he was loyal. As a survivor of the air crash he took over as captain of the depleted team and played a crucial role in rebuilding the side in the aftermath.

On being called up for National Service he was drafted into the Royal Army Service Corps as a driver. Normally he would be given a pass each weekend enabling him to turn out for United, but one week he found himself confined to his Aldershot barracks and seemingly out of United's crucial Cup tie against Birmingham. Busby had told him that if he made it to St Andrews he would play. Consumed by his passion for United he decided to go AWOL. He packed his football boots in a rucksack, clambered over the camp fence, hiked three miles over the countryside and thumbed a lift to Birmingham. He arrived in full uniform and was standing by the gate just as the United coach pulled into the car park. Bill described the look on Busby's face as 'staggered and bewildered'. Although he had already picked the team Busby was true to his word and Foulkes duly turned out for United in a thrilling 2–2 draw, with Dennis Viollet scoring both goals.

Another youngster to come off the Busby conveyor belt and make his way into the first team was Bobby Charlton. Bobby of course needs no introduction and his football exploits are well recorded. Born in Ashington, County Durham, he was originally trained to play football by his mum, Cissie, and his uncle, the legendary Newcastle United centre-forward Jackie Milburn. He joined United after winning England Schoolboy International honours and edged his way into the first team in October 1956 against, appropriately enough, Charlton Athletic, scoring twice in a 4–2 win. He was clearly a young rising star and, as subsequent events were to prove, the most famous footballer England has ever produced. It is said that everybody in the world knows at least two words of English — Bobby Charlton!

Of all the players in the Babes team, Geoff Bent is probably the least remembered. Like Eddie Colman he was a Salford lad and captained Salford Schoolboys in 1947 when they were winners of the English Schoolboys' Trophy. Like Byrne, he was one of the first Babes, joining United in 1948. Standing at 5 feet 11 inches and weighing 11 stone, he was a solidly built player. His chosen position was at left-back but he had no difficulty switching to centre-half, which he sometimes did in the junior sides. As cover for Roger Byrne he didn't have many opportunities to impress, making only twelve appearances in seven years. But when he was picked he never let the side down with his tough tackling and accurate passing of the ball. With his first-team opportunities limited he could have quite easily walked into another First Division club — Wolves, amongst other teams, had expressed their interest in the player. But with the maximum wage in force and the fact that his wife and new baby daughter were settled in their club house in Manchester he decided to stay loyal to Busby and the club. If he hadn't died at Munich it is difficult to believe he would have remained in the shadows indefinitely.

Today the physical fitness of football players is of paramount importance and smoking is regarded as strictly taboo. But back in the fifties the health dangers were largely unknown and it was considered just a part of everyday social life. Everyone seemed to have the habit in those days and the Babes were no exception. Most were regular smokers, including fitness fanatic Roger Byrne. Jimmy Murphy was a notorious chain-smoker and Tom Curry, who looked after the players' fitness, was a familiar sight strutting around Old Trafford puffing away on his pipe. Even Bobby Charlton in his early days at the club dabbled, and Duncan Edwards tried it, he said, because everyone else did. Busby, also a smoker, was known to reward his players with a packet of twenty after each game, win or lose. Smoking was certainly tolerated at Old Trafford, as can be seen in the 'Training Rules and

Instructions' booklet issued to every player upon joining the club. It states under rule number eleven: 'Smoking is strictly prohibited during training hours, and players are earnestly requested to reduce smoking to the absolute minimum on the day of the match.'

One player who certainly didn't smoke, or drink for that matter, was Liam Whelan. Busby signed the eighteen-year-old Dubliner from the famous Home Farm club in 1953. Known as Billy to his teammates, he was in every way a complete contrast to the rest of the Babes. He was a softly spoken, quiet, inoffensive lad and was never known to swear. Right from the time of his arrival in Manchester he became terribly homesick and found it hard to settle in the succession of digs provided by the club. Eventually he was invited to live at the home of Sean Dolan, who worked for the future United chairman Louis Edwards. It was there that he finally managed to settle down in what was to become his home from home.

He was deeply religious and, like Jimmy Murphy, attended Mass every day without fail. Bobby Charlton, who once shared a room with him at Mrs Watson's boarding house, bore witness to Liam's nightly Roman Catholic rituals with the rosary. Jimmy Murphy told him once, 'If you weren't such a great player, you'd make a smashing priest.' He shunned the limelight and preferred a quiet night in rather than out on the razzle-dazzle with the rest of the lads. Apart from his teammates, the only acquaintances he made during his time in Manchester were Roman Catholic priests. He had a girlfriend back home in Dublin, Ruby McCullagh, and they were due to marry in June 1958; because of his devout nature it is most unlikely that their relationship was ever consummated.

As a player he could look slow and clumsy on the football field but he was gifted with amazing skill and ball control. He was a sublime dribbler and ghosted past opponents with ease and once in shooting distance of goal he was lethal, as his record of better than a goal in every two games testifies. Apart from his lack of pace his only fault was that he didn't realise just how good he was. Because he wasn't aggressive in his play he was sometimes barracked by his own fans, which he found difficult to cope with.

After one such barracking he asked Busby to leave him out of the next game. Busby told him, 'Listen son, the time to worry is when I have a go at you.'

After an exceptional performance by Whelan in a youth tournament in Switzerland, Busby received a tentative enquiry from Brazil about his availability. Needless to say Busby discouraged further interest. Around the beginning of 1958 he was edged out of the first team by the new wonder boy, Bobby Charlton. But there can be no doubt that if Munich hadn't intervened, this talented player would have sooner or later reclaimed his place in the first team.

To augment these precocious talents Busby added the experienced Johnny Berry at outside-right. Busby bought the little winger for £25,000 from Birmingham City in 1950 after he saw him single-handedly destroy United in a game. Making his debut in September 1951 against Bolton at Burden Park, he was an ever-present member of the team for the next seven seasons, notching up nearly 300 appearances with forty-three goals.

Ray Wood signed for United as an eighteen-year-old from Darlington in 1949 for £5,000, and soon established himself as first choice goalkeeper, taking over from Reg Allen. Busby, ever ready to experiment, even tried him out as centre-forward in a few 'A' team matches where he scored a handful of goals. In December 1957 he lost his place to new signing Harry Gregg. Busby said of his goalkeeping style, 'You didn't get miracles from Ray; he was just there when it mattered.'

Other players supporting the Babes and challenging for places in the first team were full-back Ian Greaves, wing-halves Wilf McGuinness and Freddie Goodwin, centre-half Ronnie Cope and forwards Colin Webster, Alex Dawson and Mark Pearson.

Whenever United were facing a crucial game or the players were looking a bit jaded, Busby would whisk them off to the Norbreck Hydro Hotel in Blackpool. The choice of venue could possibly have had something to do with Busby having a flat a few miles up the coast in Cleveleys! The hotel had its own golf course and swimming pool and was an ideal place for the team to relax, train on the beach and recharge their batteries. Generally on these outings the players behaved themselves impeccably but on one visit things got a bit out of hand, as Dennis Viollet recalled:

One evening Matt Busby told us that we could go to a show, but stressed that he wanted us back by eleven o'clock at the latest. So off we went in high spirits to see Ted Heath's Band, who at the time were a big name in the show business world and played the type of music we all enjoyed.

As the show progressed, it soon became obvious that it was going to overrun its scheduled time and if we wanted to listen to all the concert then the manager's curfew was out of the window. David Pegg, Tommy Taylor, Duncan Edwards and myself had a little consultation along the row and the unanimous decision was to stay put. Not only did we watch the rest of the show, but the band also played a few encores making it even later in finishing and by the time we all found taxis and got back to the Norbreck it was one in the morning.

As we tiptoed into the silent, and what we thought was a deserted lobby, like a bunch of errant schoolboys, we suddenly saw trainer Tom Curry sound asleep on a chair in the corner. Obviously he had been waiting up for us. Anyway, still in high spirits someone scribbled a note saying: 'Don't wait up for us', placing it on Tom's lap before disappearing upstairs.

Despite the late night, we were all up as normal and onto the stands for training the following morning without the night before being mentioned. On our way back, however, Tom was asked: 'What time's lunch?' To which he replied that we would have little appetite for food once the Boss had spoken to us and that he wanted to see everyone in the hotel right away.

We sat like schoolboys awaiting their headmaster until Matt entered the room, slamming the door behind him. He was furious to say the least as he set about us, telling everyone that they were a disgrace, letting not only ourselves down but also the club and our supporters. He ended by threatening to drop everyone if we ever stepped out of line again. Needless to say he was never taken up on his word.

The 1954–55 campaign could be described as the calm before the storm. The Babes were improving and gaining confidence with each and every game they played. It was the season that saw Albert Scanlon, Mark Jones and Liam Whelan drafted into the first team for the occasional game and was notable for Bobby Charlton signing professional forms. They finished the season a creditable fifth in the League.

As the new 1955–56 season kicked off all the sports writers predicted a great future for Busby's exciting young team, but there were some soccer pundits who held the view — like Alan Hanson's comment in 1996 that 'you won nothing with kids' — that there was too much youth and too little experience. With only three wins in the opening eight games it seemed the critics were right. But they were soon to eat their words when suddenly everything clicked; the Babes found their feet and lost only four games in the rest of the season. By Christmas it was all over; United were on top of the table and never looked back. They romped home with the First Division title on sixty points with their nearest challengers, Wolves and Blackpool, eleven points adrift. The impact the Babes made that season was incredible and suddenly the attention of the whole country was now focused on Manchester United. There was no doubt that a new football aristocracy had been born — the Babes had come of age and were destined for something big.

The Babes' popularity captured the public's imagination like no other team had before. Their fame had spread far beyond the confines of Manchester; it encompassed the whole country and beyond. They were even celebrated in song when Trinidadian singer Edric Connor, with the backing of Ken Jones and His Music, recorded an upbeat song about the Babes to a calypso beat:

If they're playing in your town
Be sure to get to that football ground

If you do, then you'll see
Football taught by Matt Busby
At Manchester — Manchester United
A bunch of bouncing Busby Babes
They deserve to be knighted.

Winning the Championship title with an average age of twenty-two, the Babes were elevated to the status of pop stars and attracted instant recognition on the streets of Manchester. But for all their fame they were far from rich. Most of them still lived at home or in digs and earned a modest £16 per week during the season and £14 in the non-playing summer months. Their basic wage was boosted by a £2 win bonus and £1 for a draw. They also had a clause written in their contracts whereby they would be paid an additional amount depending on the size of the gate — anything above 28,000. It was not unusual to see the players look up to the stands as they emerged from the tunnel on match days to see if they could expect a little extra in their wage packets at the end of the week.

What money they did have was spent on a varied social life in the vibrant city centre of Manchester. Popular haunts they frequented included the Plaza Ballroom on Oxford Road where Jimmy Savile was the resident compere and DJ. Around the corner on Whitworth Street was the Ritz dance hall with the resident Phil Moss Band; there was also the Continental, Expresso Bongo and the Whisky a Gogo, to name a few. It was in these clubs and dance halls where they drank pints of beer together, danced to the popular music of the day — Bill Haley and his Comets, Elvis, Buddy Holly — and where, inevitably, the bachelor Babes chatted up the girls. Another venue the players often visited was the plush and prestigious members-only Cromford Club, a popular meeting place for sportsmen and television and radio stars at the time. If all this was not enough and they were hungry they would head off to their favourite restaurant, the Ping Hong on Oxford Road.

Another popular night out was a trip to the cinema and there were plenty to choose from in 1950s Manchester, including the Gaumont, Odeon and Theatre Royal. Bobby Charlton, who had not been long with United, had reason to remember the first time he accompanied established stars David Pegg and Tommy Taylor into the city centre to see a film. 'I thought I'd better behave like a professional football player,' said Bobby. 'As we got to the cinema kiosk, I said, "I'll get these lads, where are we sitting?" Tommy Taylor said, "Just get three in the best, Bob," which I did, only to find that nearly all my first week's wages had disappeared!'

Provided they behaved themselves and didn't get into trouble in pursuing their hectic and enjoyable social life, Busby would turn a blind eye. Any shenanigans that did go on were dealt with by a quiet word in the ear rather than a fine.

With the League Championship trophy back at Old Trafford and the team still improving, there seemed to be no heights that the Babes couldn't aspire to; riding on the crest of a wave they looked forward to blazing a trail into Europe in the forthcoming season and attempting something no other team had done before: winning the treble.

Chapter 3
Kid Dynamite

No story about the Busby Babes would be complete without mention of one very special and gifted young player — Duncan Edwards. Probably more words have been written and spoken about him than any other English footballer. There can be no argument that he was the most prized of the Busby Babes; he was the essence and the heart of the team and symbolic of what United stood for. Had he lived he would have gone on to become Manchester United's and England's greatest ever player. His tragic death at Munich aged just twenty-one ensured, like all those who die young and gifted, legendary status. He had fewer than five full seasons in League football but he made such an indelible impression that the passage of fifty years has been unable to erase it. Today he is still talked about in awe and his memory shows no sign of diminishing.

Duncan was born on 1 October 1936, to Sarah Anne and Gladstone Edwards, in a small Victorian terraced house at 23 Malvern Crescent, in the Midlands town of Dudley. The family later moved to Elm Road on the deprived and tough Priory Estate, where Duncan spent his formative years. He was born into a hard working-class family where there were already football connections. His father played at amateur level and his uncle played for Bolton Wanderers and had represented England in the early thirties. Like many of his contemporaries Duncan honed his footballing skills in the local streets and parks, where he spent all his time kicking a ball. If he didn't have a ball he would kick stones and when he wasn't playing the game he would talk and dream about it; he even took the ball to bed.

It is said that Duncan could kick a ball before he could walk. His mother Sarah, who died in 2003 aged ninety-three, said of her son:

Football just came naturally to him. As a boy he used to play with grown men in the street. One fella said to me: 'Mrs Edwards, you want to watch him, he'll get somewhere.' He was magic with his feet. Nobody showed him how to kick a ball, the talent was always there. He hadn't even started to walk when his dad, Gladstone, bought him a ball and he wouldn't stop kicking it around. That was the start of it. He loved football.

At the age of eleven Duncan was playing for Priory Road Junior School where his football artistry was already being noticed by the staff. One of his teachers, Mr Groves, recalled watching Duncan playing in a school match where he dominated the game. Groves said, 'He told all the other twenty-one players what to do and where to go — even the referee and linesmen! When I got home that evening, I wrote to a friend, and said: "I have just seen a boy of eleven who will one day play for England."'

In 1948, at the age of twelve, Duncan moved to Wolverhampton Street Secondary School and was soon captaining the school team. He quickly progressed to play for Dudley Schools, Worcester County and Birmingham and District, playing against boys two and three years older than him. It was around this time that Duncan wrote a school essay in which he mused about playing for England at Wembley. That essay was foretelling. On 1 April 1950, aged just thirteen, he ran out of the tunnel and onto the hallowed turf of Wembley in front of 100,000 spectators wearing the white England shirt in a schoolboy international game against Wales. After that he played in every England schoolboy international game for the next three seasons — a record that still stands today. Nothing, it seemed, could stop Duncan's meteoric rise and football scouts up and down the country began to sit up and take notice — he was an amazing prospect.

As a young teenager he had the physique of a man; he was a colossus in every sense. Standing at 5 feet 10 inches and weighing 13 stone 7 pounds, he had a chest like a barrel, the arms of a blacksmith and legs like tree trunks, and as he matured he became even stronger.

It was naturally assumed by everyone that Duncan would sign for his local team, Wolverhampton Wanderers, who were then one of the top First Division sides. The fact that he joined United and not Wolves is down to Busby's close friendship with Joe Mercer, an Arsenal player who later went on to manage Aston Villa, Manchester City and England. At the time Mercer was coaching the England schoolboys and tipped off Busby that Edwards was the best prospect of the present bunch of schoolboy internationals, and in his opinion would make a world-beater. Busby knew that Joe was a shrewd judge of young talent and on his recommendation he alerted his trusted chief scout, Joe Armstrong, to put a watch on the youngster.

Jimmy Murphy and Bert Whalley went to watch Edwards in almost every game he played and they both agreed that they had to sign this budding genius. On hearing their assessment Busby travelled to Dudley to talk to his parents, while Murphy, leaving no stone unturned, even spoke to his schoolteachers.

In the early fifties no club could legally approach a youngster before he left school and, as expected, when Duncan reached fifteen a stream of frenzied managers beat a path to his door offering him payments and inducements to join their club. However, Busby wasn't unduly concerned by these overtures as Duncan had told him, 'Manchester United is the greatest club in the world. I'd give anything to play for your team, Mr Busby.' But that did not stop their rivals from putting pressure on Duncan and his parents to change their minds. The Wolves manager, Stan Cullis, made at least two visits to his home and Bolton Wanderers did their best to entice him to sign for the Lancashire club because his cousin, Dennis Stevens, was already on their books.

Busby was sufficiently concerned by these attempts to poach the youngster from under his nose that he decided to take no chances. He immediately dispatched Jimmy Murphy and Bert Whalley to drive through the night to secure his signature. Arriving at Duncan's home at 3.30 a.m., they woke the family up. After a brief talk with his parents they asked to speak to their son. A short time later a bleary-eyed, pyjama-clad Duncan, rubbing the sleep from his eyes, walked down the stairs wondering what all the fuss was about and there and then signed for United. From that day on Duncan, a real-life Roy of the Rovers, was on his way to football stardom.

When Duncan arrived in Manchester he was put into digs with half a dozen other United youngsters who soon gave him the nickname 'Brush' because of his obsession with tidiness. On the training field Jimmy Murphy immediately began to coach and mould Edwards into the world class player he later became. But as it turned out there was little Murphy needed to teach him, and in no time he was promoted into the reserve team. Jimmy Murphy once said that 'any manager lucky enough to have big Dunc had half a team'.

He was blessed with every attribute a footballer could possibly want: physique, speed, ball control, stamina, power and courage. He was good with both feet, brilliant in the air and as an individual he could break the best organised defences; yet despite his size he could pull off the most delicate of touches with the ball. Added to this was an equable temperament that helped him cope with the pressures generated by his talent. He was always composed, nothing fazed him and he was never known to lose his temper. Everything about him epitomised all that was best in English football.

Jimmy Murphy recalled a Youth Cup game against a well-known London club in which Duncan was playing. The match had hardly got underway when a heckling opposition supporter shouted down to Murphy from the stands, 'Hey, Murphy, where's your so-called wonder boy Edwards?' Jimmy didn't turn a hair, said nothing and carried on watching the game. A few minutes later Duncan won a tackle on the halfway line and powered his way towards the opposition's goal with defenders bouncing off his massive frame like ping-pong balls. From thirty yards out he hit a blistering shot that was in the back of the net before the keeper had time to react. Jimmy turned around, looked at the heckling fan straight in the eyes and said, 'That's Edwards!'

On Easter Monday 1953, Duncan was on ground duties at Old Trafford when Matt Busby walked over and told him, 'Get your boots on, you're playing for the first team against Cardiff.' He was just fifteen years and 285 days old, the youngest ever professional footballer to play in the First Division. After his League debut he hardly played in a reserve game again. Two years later, in April 1955, he broke another record by becoming the youngest player to be capped for England, a record only beaten by Michael Owen of Liverpool forty-five years later. His debut was marked by thrashing Scotland 7–2 at Wembley.

Reputations meant nothing to Duncan and he feared no one; he knew he was special, but not in a big headed way. The late great Jackie Milburn used to tell the story of the day he first came up against the sixteen-year-old in a game. He remembers standing beside him on the pitch just before kick-off and listened as Duncan told him, 'I know that you are a great player Mr Milburn, and that you have a big reputation, but it means nothing at all to me. Today I am not going to allow you a kick at the ball.' Milburn said, 'The thing was, Duncan was absolutely true to his word, I hardly did get a kick throughout that game and United won 5–2. I just could not believe how mature this young kid was, and what ability and self-belief he had.' After the match Duncan walked over to Jackie, sportingly shook his hand, and said, 'Thanks for the game, chief.'

Another story that illustrates his fearless nature occurred in a game, against West Brom in 1957 when he came up against Maurice Setters, a tough and abrasive winger. As Duncan tried to take a throw-in Setters walked over and faced up to him nose-to-nose. Duncan looked him straight in the eyes and without any viciousness pushed out his chest and sent Setters reeling backwards, landing on his arse. Needless to say Setters didn't bother him for the rest of the game.

Duncan was now gaining the reputation of a player you didn't mess with. In an England v. Wales game at Ninian Park in Cardiff, Jimmy Murphy, in his other role as the Welsh team manager, was in the changing room prior to the kick-off giving his team the run down on the opposing players and how to counter them. When he had finished, Reg Davies, the Newcastle centre-forward, said to Jimmy, 'But Boss, you haven't said anything about this bloke Duncan Edwards, what do you want us to do about him?' Murphy paused for a moment, put his arm around his shoulder and whispered in his ear, 'Keep out of his fucking way, son. Keep out of his way.'

In George Best's day there were copious amounts of alcohol and sex, but none of this applied to Duncan. He filled his time between playing and training by going to the cinema, sometimes as often as three times a week, according to his mother. Another of his interests, along with some of his teammates, was Sunday afternoon trips out to Ringway Airport on the southern edge of the city. There he would spend many a happy hour in the airport drinking tea served by his favourite waitress Amy, who, although in her seventies, used to entertain the players with her skipping rope. Despite his fascination with all things aeronautical, Duncan had a pathological fear of flying and preferred whenever possible to keep both his feet firmly placed on terra firma.

Matt Busby, never one to single out any one his players as the greatest, said of Edwards:

Duncan was the player who had everything. He was so big, so strong, so confident and so young. We used to look at players in training to see if we might have to get them to concentrate more on their kicking, perhaps, or their heading or ball control, whatever. We looked at Duncan, right at the start, and gave up trying to spot flaws in his game.

Apart from anything else, he could move up field and lash in goals when we needed them. John Charles was a giant of a player, a giant with great skill. But John and Duncan were different. Of the two, Duncan was the more powerful player. He used to move up the field, brushing players aside. Nothing could stop him and nothing unnerved him.

The bigger the occasion, the better he liked it. He had no nerves before a game. He was like George Best in that respect. While other players would have to be pacing up and down a dressing room, rubbing their legs, doing exercises and looking for ways to pass the time, Duncan, and George later, was always calm. They would glance through a programme or get changed casually and wait without a trace of tension.

I remember a game at Highbury, when I brought Ronnie Cope into the team and I told Duncan, who was only a boy himself, to keep an eye on him. Believe me. You would have thought Duncan had been a professional for twenty years that day.

He was a good type of lad too. Even in those days, when football followers were not what they became later with regard to wanting to be with players socially, you still had people who waited for them. But Duncan did not want to know about the high life. He just wanted to play and go to his digs or go home. He lived for his football.

In this modern age of millionaire footballing superstars it must be remembered that Edwards earned just £16 a week during the season, reduced to £14 in the out of season summer months. But as a rising star he bolstered his meagre income in modest ways, advertising Dextrosol glucose tablets, which claimed to be 'a natural source of energy which you could rely on anytime, anywhere'. Whether Duncan ever used or needed the tablets is not recorded. Added to that was £4 10s he was paid for his weekly football column in the *Manchester Evening Chronicle*. He also had the use of a sponsored Raleigh racing bike which he put to good use cycling to and from the ground. On one occasion his bike got him into hot water. It was on one Saturday evening after a derby game at Old Trafford in 1955 where their rivals City thrashed them 5–0. As usual, after the game Duncan jumped on his bike to cycle back to his digs in nearby Stretford, when he was booked on Chester Road by an over-zealous police officer for riding without lights. On the Monday morning he was hauled before the magistrates and fined 10s. But worse was to come: arriving at Old

Trafford, Busby, who had got wind of the incident, called him into his office and fined him two weeks wages for bringing the name of Manchester United into disrepute!

In scenes reminiscent of a state funeral, five thousand people lined the streets of Dudley to pay a tearful farewell to their own local hero. On his headstone is an etched image showing him in his England football strip, holding a ball above his head as if ready for a throw-in. An inscription reads: 'A Day of Memory Sad to Recall, Without Farewell He Left Us All'. When he died Duncan Edwards had the world at his feet and was barely on the threshold of his career that would have undoubtedly made him the greatest footballer of his generation. Fifty years on the fans still come in pilgrimage to his graveside, singly and in groups. Whenever Manchester United have a game in the Midlands it is not unusual to find his headstone draped with United scarves along with red and white blooms placed at the graveside the following day.

Just before Duncan flew to Belgrade on that fateful trip he had just handed over to the publishers his manuscript *Tackle Soccer This Way* — tapped out on his Remington typewriter in Mrs Watson's digs — in which he offers young budding footballers hundreds of tips. It was printed after his death word for word as he wrote it. A line from the book sums up perfectly the maturity, character and sportsmanship of one so young: 'Always respect the referee and be reasonable at all times'. It is difficult to believe that those words could be spoken by the megastar players of today.

Duncan had recently become engaged to Molly Leach, a Manchester girl he had met on one of his many Sunday afternoon jaunts to Ringway Airport. He had also recently bought a car — despite the fact he couldn't drive — and every Sunday morning he and Molly could be seen outside his digs polishing what was his pride and joy. He had so much to look forward to. Sadly it all came to an abrupt and tragic end in a snow-covered field in Germany.

Although Duncan Edwards will always be associated with Manchester United and the Busby Babes, his hometown of Dudley is still very proud of its very own local hero and has never forgotten him; today he has become the town's main tourist attraction and hundreds come each year to enquire after him. In recent years the local authority has seen fit to erect a life-size bronze statue in the main shopping square as a permanent reminder of the town's legendary son.

In a corner of St Francis' Church, which Duncan attended as a boy and where his funeral took place, stand two stained-glass windows erected in his memory. One shows Duncan in the Manchester United strip he wore for the last time in the European Cup match against Red Star Belgrade; the other depicts him in the England shirt he proudly wore in eighteen internationals. A short walk from Elm Road, where Duncan grew up, stands the Duncan Edwards pub, once known as the Wren's Nest. It was in the car park of the Nest where Duncan as a boy incessantly kicked the ball against the pub wall, much to the annoyance of the landlord.

Fifty years on we are left to speculate what he would have achieved if Munich hadn't intervened. Barring serious injury he would have probably gone on to be the most capped player for England, beating Billy Wright's record of 105 appearances. He was at the time the youngest player to be picked for England; but for his tragic death he would have most certainly grown to be the oldest. At the age of twenty-nine and arguably still at his peak, it would most likely have been Duncan Edwards and not Bobby Moore who led out the England team at Wembley for the 1966 World Cup final.

All this of course is pure speculation, we will never truly know. But what is certain is that English football was robbed of an exceptionally rare talent, the like of which we may never see again. That is probably the saddest legacy of Munich.

Over the years many have been compared to Edwards — Terry Venables, Kevin Beattie, the former Manchester United captain Bryan Robson, and more recently Liverpool and England international Steven Gerrard. But with no disrespect to these talented players, none of them have come anywhere close to the class and genius of Edwards.

Duncan's mother, in a television documentary a few years before her death, said, 'You know, I never told Duncan he was great, but he was. I never told him I loved him, but I did.' So too did a whole generation of fans, not just in Manchester, but all over the country and beyond. As Frank Taylor, the only sports writer to survive Munich, said, 'So long, Dunc. It was great while it lasted.'

In his book *United, Matt and Me*, Jimmy Murphy says of Duncan: 'If I shut my eyes I can see him now. Those pants hitched up, the wild leaps of boyish enthusiasm as he came out of the tunnel, the tremendous power of his tackle — always fair but fearsome — the immense power on the ball. He played wing-half, centre-half, centre-forward and inside-forward with consummate ease. When I hear Mohammed Ali proclaim "I am the greatest" I have to smile. You see, the greatest of them all was an English footballer named Duncan Edwards.'

Chapter 4
Passport to Europe

It was Henri Delaunay, the secretary of the French Football Federation, who first mooted the idea of a European Cup competition as far back as 1927, but in the end because of the problems of arranging extra fixtures, poor air links and the lack of floodlighting the proposal fizzled out. The concept was revived once again by Gabriel Hanot, a former French international and editor of the influential French sports paper *L'Equipe*. The idea arose after he read an article in an English newspaper that Wolverhampton Wanderers were the best team in the world after 'rolling over' Spartak Moscow and Honved of Hungary in friendly matches. This boast irked Hanot and he countered: 'We had better wait until the Wolves travel to Moscow and Budapest to proclaim their invincibility; but if the English are so sure about their hegemony in football, then this is the time to create a European tournament.' Hanot believed that such a competition would finally settle the debate of who really was the best in Europe.

Hanot unveiled his proposal on 16 December 1954. His initial plan was for a league competition involving sixteen of Europe's leading clubs. Games would be played midweek under floodlights. However, his plan ran into an immediate problem: that of fixture congestion. Clubs and their national associations were doubtful about fitting in yet another competition alongside their own domestic leagues. Most of the clubs consulted favoured a knockout format, to reduce the number of games played. With that in mind, Hanot redrafted his proposal so that there would be home and away legs, with the winner on aggregate going on to the next round until the final.

In April 1955 eighteen of the top European clubs met in Paris to iron out the final details and it was agreed that the competition would start the following season (1955–56). Some of the clubs, although not current domestic champions, were invited to take part in the inaugural season based on their past performance. But the rules would change for the 1956–57 competition, when only the national champions and the cup holders would be allowed to enter.

Chelsea, who won the League Championship for the first time in 1954–55, were invited to compete in the first competition, but the xenophobic secretary of the Football League, Alan Hardaker — who once told a reporter, 'I don't like Europe, too many wops and dagoes for my liking' — would have none of it. In his view there were already enough games in the English domestic season, and if teams were going to travel to Europe to fulfil fixtures then it would, he felt, have an adverse effect on the home game. He certainly lacked the vision that the tournament was the opening of a door, showing British players the technical skills of the Continentals and also that it would be a marvellous money-spinner for the best clubs. He put pressure on the Chelsea board and told them in no uncertain terms to turn down the offer. The club did exactly what he asked.

It was no surprise when Manchester United won the Championship in 1956 that a letter arrived at Old Trafford from the Football League forbidding United to take part in the competition. But Busby, a visionary far ahead of his time, was made of sterner stuff and had no intention of missing this golden opportunity to broaden the club's horizons. His young team had beaten the best at home and now he wanted to spread the name of Manchester United beyond the confines of England and beat the best Europe had to offer. With the support of the Football Association and the United directors, he made the bold decision to accept the invitation to compete, despite Hardaker's opposition. Busby, his players and the fans never doubted for a moment that it was the right thing to do.

Manchester United's assault on Europe began on 12 September 1956 when they faced the Belgium champions Anderlecht under the floodlights of the Astrid Park Stadium in Brussels. They were managed by the Lancastrian Bill Gormlie who at one time kept goal for Blackburn Rovers. On paper they were considered to be no pushovers, having been Belgian champions seven times since the war. In a game that could have gone either way United took the advantage, with goals from Dennis Viollet and Tommy Taylor. But the man of the match was without doubt Jackie Blanchflower, who came in to replace the injured Duncan Edwards; his superlative display of football set Brussels alight that night and was the main factor in United's victory. But the game gave no hint of the drama that was to follow in the return leg at Maine Road.

Three days later it was back to the business of league football with newly promoted Sheffield Wednesday the visitors at Old Trafford. The press speculated before the game that the United players would be exhausted after their midweek excursion to the Continent, and Busby knew only too well that a poor performance would bring contempt from Hardaker and others not in favour of the European competition. But he needn't have worried: the Babes turned on their magic and dispatched Wednesday back over the Pennines at the end of a resounding 4–1 defeat. The following week they beat neighbours Manchester City 2–0 in an emotive derby with Liam Whelan and Dennis Viollet the scorers. These two victories kept United at the top of the table and on course for a second Championship title.

With the floodlights at Old Trafford not yet erected, it was back to Maine Road on Wednesday 26 September to face Anderlecht in the second leg. It had rained heavily throughout the day but that did nothing to dampen the high spirits of the 43,000 chanting fans packed inside the stadium. The match they were about to see turned out to be the most memorable game ever played in the history of the European Cup competition and has since become part of Manchester United folklore. Before they left the dressing room Busby told his players, 'Go out and enjoy it.' That night they did exactly that.

The Babes ran out of the tunnel onto the sodden pitch to the deafening roar of the excited home crowd. Anderlecht had travelled over truly believing they could wipe out the two-goal deficit inflicted in the first leg and win the round, but they were in for a shock. By the end of the ninety minutes they wished that they had never made the journey.

With Duncan Edwards back in the side the Babes were at full strength. From the first blast of the whistle United took the game to the Belgians and showed them no mercy with a punishing display of footballing brilliance. Inside ten minutes Tommy Taylor opened the scoring with a stunning header, and followed it up with a second before Dennis Viollet took over, scoring a devastating hat-trick. When the referee blew for half-time United were 5–0 up!

If anyone thought that United were going to ease up in the second half and take a back seat they were very much mistaken. They came out fired up and continued where they had left off, with Tommy Taylor putting away a sixth goal to complete his hat-trick. Liam Whelan was next, followed by another from Dennis Viollet. Even Johnny Berry was not to be denied when he too fired one home. Leading 9–0, the rapturous fans were chanting, 'WE WANT TEN, WE WANT TEN', and as if to oblige Liam Whelan smashed the ball into the back of the net to score his second and United's tenth goal. It was incredible. The only forward not to get his name on the scoresheet that night was David Pegg. As the victorious Babes trooped off the pitch they were applauded all the way to the dressing room by the Anderlecht players. That night they could have beaten any team in the world.

After the game Busby said, 'It was the greatest thrill in a lifetime of soccer, it was the finest exhibition of teamwork I have ever seen from any team, club or international. It was as near perfect football as anyone could wish to see.'

Jeff Mermans, the Anderlecht captain, unaware that Liam Whelan was Irish, asked, 'Why don't they pick this whole team for

England?' Even the match referee Mervyn Griffiths was moved to comment, 'I have refereed teams all over Europe but I have never seen football like United displayed and the precision of their passing was remarkable. Even after they had scored their tenth goal they were still running as if the game had just started.'

The headlines in the following morning newspapers said it all: 'UNITED THRASH ANDERLECHT', 'SOCCER MASSACRE' and 'BUSBY'S BOYS BANG IN TEN!'

Three days later, still on a high, they travelled to the capital to face Arsenal at Highbury, and in front of 62,000 spectators had little difficulty beating the Londoners 2–1 with goals from Johnny Berry and Liam Whelan. A week later Charlton Athletic came to Old Trafford to find a depleted United team without Byrne, Edwards, Taylor and Blanchflower — all having been called up for international duty. Despite an under-strength side they easily won the game 4–2 with Bobby Charlton scoring twice on his debut. The victory extended United's unbeaten run to thirty-one games — beating Burnley's 1920–21 record — and set the standard for their chasing rivals.

It was another trip to Maine Road on the evening of 17 October to confront the German champions Borussia Dortmund in the next round of the European Cup. A crowd of 75,598 packed into the ground — the biggest attendance seen at Maine Road since 1934 — and all were hoping for another goal bonanza. But it wouldn't be that easy — although the German side were older than their counterparts they certainly didn't lack in ability and experience. United got off to a whirlwind start, leading 3–0 after thirty-five minutes with two goals from Viollet and a gifted own goal from Burgsmueller. However in the second half the Babes lost their poise, allowing Dortmund to come back to score two late goals due to silly defensive errors. United trooped off the pitch wondering if that one-goal margin would be enough to keep them in the competition when they travelled over to Germany for the return leg.

When Everton came to Old Trafford on the following Saturday they turned the form book on its head and surprised everyone by thrashing United 5–2, ending their record unbeaten run. By a strange coincidence it was Everton who were the last side to win at Old Trafford way back in March 1955. The players and the fans were shell-shocked by the result. Busby, concerned that his players were becoming tired and jaded after playing all these extra games, decided to whisk the team off to the Norbreck Hydro in Blackpool for a change of scene and well-deserved break before their next European encounter.

It was a refreshed United team that travelled to the Ruhr, deep in the heart of Germany, on 21 November for the second leg against Borussia Dortmund. The German club had astonishingly erected floodlights at the ground in just three weeks to enable the tie to go ahead. On the day of the match the weather was freezing and the playing surface was like an ice rink. Having brought no rubber studs with them, team trainer Tom Curry did a quick cobbling job in the changing room, fitting short studs on the player's boots. It helped but they still struggled to keep their footing on the icy surface. In front of 45,000 spectators, including thousands of British army conscripts stationed in West Germany, the Babes managed to keep the gold-shirted Germans at bay to earn a creditable no-score draw and a place in the quarter final against Spanish champions Athletico Bilbao.

Sandwiched between the European Cup games leading up to the New Year, United won all but one of their League fixtures, including a 6–1 thrashing of Newcastle United at Old Trafford. Their one defeat against Birmingham City at St Andrews did nothing to dent their title aspirations and by mid-January they were six points clear of Tottenham Hotspur with forty-eight points. In the FA Cup they progressed to the fifth round with wins over Hartlepool and Wrexham.

It was a cold and frosty morning when the team, officials and pressmen boarded an old British European Airways Dakota at Ringway Airport, bound for Bilbao. If the Babes thought they were leaving a cold, wet and miserable Manchester and flying off to sunny Spain they were in for a shock. The flight out was rough and turbulent and as the aircraft crabbed along the western coast of France the heating packed in. Harold Hardman, the 75-year-old club chairman, began to shiver in the freezing conditions and was clearly unwell. It later transpired that he had suffered a mild stroke, which resulted in him being rushed to hospital when they landed. The chairman was not the only one to suffer — both Mark Jones and Liam Whelan endured bouts of airsickness, and Duncan Edwards, although a giant on the football field, was not the best flyer in the world and became increasingly ill as the flight progressed.

The Dakota safely touched down at Bordeaux for refuelling, and after the heating system was fixed the party were quickly on their way. Arriving over Bilbao, Captain Riley circled, having difficulty locating the airport in the snowstorm. He broadcast over the cabin tannoy — to the consternation of all on board — for everyone to keep a look out for the runway! Riley was unaware that due to the weather conditions the airport was closed, and it was only when an Embassy official heard the drone of the engines overhead that he rushed to the airport and had it reopened. With that Captain Riley managed to put the aircraft down on the runway in a blizzard and taxied to a stop in front of a huddle of airport buildings. Eddie Colman stepped out of the aircraft, stood at the top of the stairs and, gazing at the falling snow, exclaimed, 'Bloody hell! Just like Salford!'

The hotel accommodation provided was more than adequate but the hot and spicy food served up did not agree with some of the players, especially Tommy Taylor who came down with a stomach complaint. With the fear of being pulled from the team he said nothing to Busby, preferring to suffer in silence until he recovered. It had rained incessantly since their arrival and on the day of the match the playing surface resembled a swamp with the line markings non-existent. Busby feared the match would be postponed, but after several pitch inspections the match officials declared the pitch playable — it was the worst conditions that United had ever been asked to play in.

Huge flakes of snow drifted down from a leaden sky as United ran out of the tunnel into the Sans Mames Stadium in their changed strip of unfamiliar royal blue shirts. Bilbao, playing in their traditional red and white stripes, had lost only one game on their home ground in three years. With five Spanish internationals in their line-up they were a formidable side and soon showed their class by tearing United apart from the start to lead 3–0 at half-time.

In the dressing room Busby gave his players a pep talk to gee them up in his usual calming tone. But as soon as he had left the room and was out of earshot, the fire-breathing Jimmy Murphy laid into the team and gave them one of his arm-waving, inspirational and uplifting sermons. It seemed to have the desired effect and within eight minutes of the restart they were back in the game with goals from Tommy Taylor and Dennis Viollet. Alarmingly, Bilbao came back, scoring twice, caused in the main by United's slack defending. Trailing 5–2 with the time ticking remorselessly on it seemed United were finished. How could they possibly hope to score four clear goals at home in the second leg to win the tie on aggregate? It looked to everyone that United were about to bow out of the European Cup in their first season.

Then, with less than five minutes remaining, Liam Whelan gathered a pass from Duncan Edwards on the halfway line and set off on a forty-yard run through the sea of mud and snow towards the Bilbao goal. Tommy Taylor, sprinting alongside, screamed at him for all he was worth to pass the ball. But Liam was having none of it; he kept the ball glued to his feet, determined to score. Weaving effortlessly past five bewildered defenders, he lifted the ball out of the clinging mud and blasted it into the top left-hand corner of the goal, silencing the screaming Bilbao fans. It was an absolute once-in-a-lifetime cracker of a goal; no one in the world could have scored one better. On the sidelines Busby and Murphy were jumping up and down hugging each other, delirious with joy.

When the team arrived at Bilbao Airport to travel home the following day there was a stark omen of what was to come in Munich a year later. It had now snowed continuously for twenty-four hours with the inevitable result that their BEA Dakota, left on the apron overnight, was covered in a blanket of snow and ice. On his arrival at the airport, Captain Riley took one look at his stricken aircraft and proclaimed they wouldn't be flying back that day. Busby, aware of the need to return home to fulfil their League fixture against Sheffield Wednesday on the coming Saturday and avoid the wrath of Hardaker's Football League, ordered his players to clear the snow.

It was an incredible sight as the players, officials, airport staff and even the pressmen marched out to the aircraft with brooms and shovels over their shoulders to sweep the wings clear of snow. It was lunchtime when the party finally took off, leaving the blizzards of sunny Spain behind. But the homebound flight proved to be even worse than the flight out, with the old Dakota running headlong into a gale. As they approached Jersey for their refuelling stop a gusting crosswind almost put the aircraft down short of the cliff-top runway, which did nothing to settle the nerves or stomachs of the petrified passengers. But Captain Riley, who had no doubt experienced this countless times, put the aircraft safely down for a bumpy landing. When they finally arrived back in Manchester it was a very relieved party that trooped off the aircraft.

After the trials of the nightmare journey to and from Bilbao and the energy-sapping conditions of the pitch, it was a fatigued and under-par team that crossed the Pennines to face Sheffield Wednesday at Hillsborough in the League, where the Owls showed them no mercy, easily beating them 2–0. The following week they were back at Maine Road facing Manchester City in a highly charged derby match. The players had now recovered their poise and easily dispatched the Blues 4–2, with Edwards, Taylor, Whelan and Viollet the goal scorers. Now all their thoughts turned to the upcoming European game against Bilbao in the second leg. Could they, the press and supporters asked, wipe out that two-goal deficit and win through to their first European Cup semi-final?

On 6 February, a date that a year later would be seared into the memory of United fans forever, the Babes returned to Maine Road to face Bilbao in the second leg. Their confident manager declared to the press before the game, 'No team in the world can beat us by three clear goals.' How wrong he was.

From the kick-off United took the game to Bilbao, eager to pull back the much-needed goals. The Spaniards, two goals up on aggregate from the first leg, organised their defence and were determined to give nothing away; knowing exactly what to expect from the United forwards they did their best to slow the game down at every opportunity. As the minutes ticked towards half-time with no sign of a breakthrough, an agitated, chain-smoking Busby waved Duncan Edwards forward to lend his power to the attack. It did the trick, when three minutes before the interval he carved his way through the middle of the defence like a tank and unleashed a blistering shot towards the Bilbao goal, only to see it blocked by the despairing foot of Jesus Garay. Dennis Viollet, the undisputed king of half-chances, raced in and, pouncing on the rebound, smacked the ball past the grasping fingers of the goalkeeper to open the scoring.

Within minutes of the restart, both Dennis Viollet and Liam Whelan had the ball in the back of the net, but the referee, right up with play, ruled both the goals offside, to howls of protest from the fans who felt their team were being robbed. United, undaunted, continued to pile on the pressure and were rewarded in the seventieth minute when Tommy Taylor blasted an unstoppable thunderbolt to level the tie. The noise from the fans was phenomenal as they cranked up the volume, urging the Babes on to get the vital winning goal.

Bilbao now began to panic and, losing their composure, pulled everyone back to thwart the onslaught. With just five minutes remaining, and a replay in Paris looking the most likely outcome, Tommy Taylor streaked down the right wing with Garay chasing him like a long-lost brother. Reaching the corner flag he delivered an inch-perfect pass to Johnny Berry, who slammed the game-winning ball home.

Maine Road erupted with a crescendo of sound that must have been heard for miles. On the touchline Busby and Murphy, hugging each other, did a jig of joy as the fans invaded the pitch. It had been an unforgettable and sensational night, but above all it was Tommy Taylor's night — probably his greatest game since joining the club. With so much local interest, the result was even flashed up on cinema screens all across the city to the cheers of the patrons.

The *Daily Herald*'s George Follows described the game as 'the greatest football match I have ever seen, the greatest football crowd

I have ever heard, and the greatest centre-forward display I have ever seen'. The headline to Henry Rose's report in the *Daily Express* exclaimed, 'THE GREATEST VICTORY IN SOCCER HISTORY'.

Three days later, with hardly time to get their breath back, United entertained Arsenal at Old Trafford and sent them packing back home to London on the end of a 6–2 thrashing and in so doing left them well clear at the top of the First Division. The following week it was back to FA Cup action, with a 1–0 victory over Everton at Old Trafford earning them a quarter-final tie against Bournemouth. Flying high in both domestic competitions they now looked forward with eagerness to their trip to Spain, with the belief that they could overcome Real Madrid in the first leg and halfway to booking their place in their first European Cup final.

From the moment they touched down in Madrid the Babes were feted like movie stars, with almost a hundred press photographers amongst the hordes waiting for them at the airport. Real Madrid was classed at the time as the greatest club side in Europe, if not the world. They boasted some of the most gifted players of the era, such as Alfredo di Stefano, the poor boy from Argentina, whose skilful feet had made him a peseta millionaire. Playing on the left wing was Francisco Gento, whose electrifying speed down the touchline earned him the nickname 'El motorbike' by the Madrid fans. There was also the skilful French international Raymond Kopa, and at the back they had Marquitos — a tough no-nonsense defender who took no prisoners. Altogether the star-studded side played slick artistic football totally different from the English style of play and United knew they would have their work cut out trying to tame the European Cup holders.

United ran out of the tunnel into the sapping heat of the magnificent Bernabéu stadium to the roar from a massive 135,000 fanatical crowd. It turned out to be a torrid game with some cruel and violent tackling from the ruthless Real players, with Marquitos the worst culprit. With fourteen fouls in the first seven minutes and with the Dutch referee doing little about it, the English press dubbed the game 'Murder in Madrid'.

For an hour, Real penned back United in defence as wave after wave of di Stefano-inspired attacks swept towards their goal, but Roger Byrne and Jackie Blanchflower, playing their hearts out, managed to keep their forwards at bay, allowing Viollet, Berry and Pegg to make the occasional sweeping raids into the Spanish half.

Real's breakthrough came in the sixtieth minute when Rial's diving header from a Gento cross hit the back of the net to open the scoring. Fifteen minutes later di Stefano added another, causing the stadium to shake with the thunderous noise of the ecstatic Spanish crowd. But it was United who was galvanised by the frenzied roar and they swept forward in search of a much-needed goal. Eight minutes from time, the Babes dramatically pulled the score back to 2–1 through a Tommy Taylor header. But Real were to have the last word when, in the dying moments of the game, Kopa flicked a ball to Mateos who shot home.

George Follows, in his match report for the *Daily Herald*, criticised Madrid's underhanded tactics: 'They hacked, slashed, kicked and wrestled their way to victory . . . their defenders committed nearly every crime in the football calendar to extract the venom from the Red Devil's attack. Referee Leo Horn weakly allowed the soccer skulduggery to continue to the truly bitter end.'

The battered and bruised players flew home for a League game against Luton Town, coming away the victors with two goals from in-form Tommy Taylor. From that day on United remained unbeaten in the League for the rest of the season, winning a second consecutive Championship. In the FA Cup they beat Bournemouth in the sixth round and Birmingham City in the semi-final to book their place at Wembley against Aston Villa in May.

With the new floodlighting system completed at Old Trafford, United were ready to host their first European Cup tie against Real Madrid in the second leg. But could they, the sporting press and the supporters asked, put on the same sort of performance as they did against Bilbao and overturn the 3–1 deficit?

From the kick-off United went on a non-stop assault on the Real Madrid goal but were unable to penetrate their resolute defence. Real were quite happy to soak up the pressure before countering in spectacular fashion, when di Stefano split the United defence with a brilliant back-heeled pass to Kopa who darted in to put the ball past Ray Wood. Five minutes later they went further ahead when the electric Gento sped down the left wing and his cross was touched home by Rial.

The Babes, to their credit, refused to accept defeat and continued to press forward, with Duncan Edwards running all over the field cajoling his teammates. The game, like the first leg, was a torrid affair and tempers soon became frayed with some malicious tackles handed out by the Spaniards. Throughout the game the Real defenders found it impossible to contain Tommy Taylor and did all they could to thwart his aerial attacks, even resorting to pulling him down by his shirt, with the referee totally blind to the blatant fouling.

In the end the Babes' continual pressure paid off when Tommy Taylor managed to pull a goal back after sixty-one minutes, followed by another from Bobby Charlton five minutes from time. To counter United's incessant attacks, the Spaniards resorted to all sorts of underhanded tactics to slow the game down and wasted time at every opportunity. When Mateos collapsed in a heap near his goalmouth following a collision and refused to get up, Roger Byrne and Duncan Edwards, not wanting the game to lose momentum, physically dragged him off the pitch to get the match restarted. In the end Real withstood the assault and held on for a 2–2 draw and a 5–3 aggregate victory.

The final whistle left the 60,000 Old Trafford crowd stunned and silent with their European Cup dream in tatters. The truth was that Real Madrid, despite their rough play and time-wasting tactics, were the better side and deserved to win. It was only the Babes' inexperience in European competition that had let them down. In their first season in the competition they were the only team that came anywhere close to toppling the mighty Madrid, who went on to lift the trophy.

Playing in Europe had been a great success; everybody had enjoyed it — Busby, the players and the supporters. No one doubted that next year they could go all the way. Despite the disappointment United now concentrated all their efforts on the League and FA Cup double — a feat last achieved by Aston Villa sixty years earlier in 1897. Having secured the League Championship, the only team that stood in their way was Aston Villa in the FA Cup final. Villa had finished mid-table in the league and were certainly the underdogs on the day, but as the history of the FA Cup has shown, there were some surprises in store. Busby said that when he came downstairs on the morning of the final he had never been more sure of victory before in all his football life. But what he could not foresee was the crucial role Villa's Peter McParland would play in the game.

The United team sheet read: Ray Wood, Bill Foulkes, Roger Byrne, Eddie Colman, Jackie Blanchflower, Duncan Edwards, Johnny Berry, Liam Whelan, Tommy Taylor, David Pegg and Bobby Charlton (who came in for the injured Viollet).

Within six minutes of the kick-off United's hopes of winning the double were dashed when Aston Villa's outside-left Peter McParland headed the ball into the United keeper's hands. Ray Wood advanced from the goal line to clear the ball up field but McParland continued racing forwards and flattened the goalkeeper with a shoulder charge, leaving him prostrate on the ground with a smashed cheekbone and concussion. In today's game it would have been a blatant foul and McParland would have been dismissed, but in those days charging the goalkeeper was accepted as part of the game.

Ray Wood was stretchered off and with no substitutes allowed in those days Jackie Blanchflower pulled on the keeper's jersey and deputised in goal. Duncan Edwards took over at centre-half with Liam Whelan dropping back to take his place in the half-back line. Down to ten men, United fought valiantly and managed to keep the game goalless at half-time. In the second half Ray Wood bravely returned to the field to play on the right wing. Suffering from double vision and concussion, he was incapable of hitting a bull's arse with a banjo. Even with that advantage it took Villa an hour to beat Blanchflower with two goals within five minutes of each other (both scored, ironically, by the villain of the first half, Peter McParland). United came back and threw everything they had at Villa, and with ten minutes remaining Tommy Taylor gave them some hope when he scored with a header. Throwing caution to the wind, Busby waved Ray Wood back into goal to release Blanchflower, in a desperate attempt to save the game. Roger Byrne urged his players on to snatch the equaliser in the dying moments but all to no avail; United crashed out of the FA Cup within an ace of winning the coveted double.

In the changing room Busby told his disappointed players that he and the club were proud of everything they had achieved and not to worry. He confidently predicted, 'We'll be back at Wembley next year.' Busby never said a truer word, but sadly most of those faces gathered around him would be missing, having been overtaken in the meantime by the tragic events at Munich.

Chapter 5
The Last Season

In the summer of 1957, just before the new season got underway, Busby took his players over to Germany to play a few friendly matches as a warm-up for a fresh assault on the League, FA Cup and European Cup. Although Busby knew his team was capable of lifting all three prizes, his main aim was to achieve a hat-trick of League title wins as Huddersfield Town did in the twenties and Arsenal in the thirties — both sides created and managed by the legendary Herbert Chapman.

The Babes' last domestic season got off to a great start. They secured eleven points from the first six games, scoring a remarkable twenty-two goals and conceding only five, putting them two points clear at the top of the table. On this early showing United looked invincible, with the fans and pundits freely predicting that this was the season they would pull off the treble. But suddenly, for no perceptible reason, the wheels came off their title challenge when on 14 September they were thrashed 4–0 by their bogey team Bolton Wanderers at Burden Park. This was quickly followed by defeats to Blackpool, Wolves, Portsmouth and West Bromwich. It was as if the stress and strain of the previous season's campaign had suddenly caught up with the Babes, causing them to lose their poise and impetus. The sporting press, used to reporting nothing but success from the United camp, began to ask questions. But Busby didn't panic; hoping it was just a temporary hiatus, he decided to wait and see if they returned to their winning ways before taking any drastic action.

In the European Cup competition they fared much better, easing their way through the preliminary round with an emphatic 6–0 victory against Shamrock Rovers at Dalymount Park in Dublin, where Liam Whelan put on a dazzling display against his fellow countrymen, scoring two goals; Tommy Taylor put away another two, with one apiece from wingers Johnny Berry and David Pegg. In the return leg at Old Trafford the fans were expecting another Anderlecht-style goal glut, but to their credit the Irish champions scored twice against a complacent United before eventually going down 3–2.

Their next European encounter was against Czechoslovakian champions Dukla Prague at Old Trafford. Dukla were a well-disciplined army side with a brace of internationals and came over to Manchester in no mood to give anything away. The Babes struggled for over an hour to find a way through the solid Czech defence, but a twelve-minute goal blitz late in the second half saw them take the first leg 3–0 in front of 60,000 delirious fans. However, Busby and his players were under no illusions that they were in for one hell of a game on Dukla's home territory.

It was cold, dank and dismal when the United players ran out onto the pitch in the compact army stadium situated in the hills overlooking Prague. It didn't help their confidence to see the terraces packed with thousands of khaki-clad Czech army conscripts, which gave the stadium the appearance of a military parade ground. Although United were outplayed for much of the game, inspirational performances from little Eddie Colman and David Pegg managed to keep Dukla's score down to 1–0. But it didn't matter; winning 3–1 aggregate, United were through to the quarter-final against Red Star Belgrade.

The following day fog over much of England prevented the United party from boarding their BEA Viscount to fly back home to Manchester. After some hasty rearrangements they managed to find seats on a KLM flight to Amsterdam and reached home by taking the ferry from the Hook of Holland to Harwich and then travelling by train to Manchester. The players were shattered by the nightmare journey and after a few hours sleep they were on the road again to play Birmingham in the League, where they managed to come away with a draw.

Playing midweek European Cup games on the Continent and getting the team back in time to fulfil their domestic league fixtures was an ever-present problem for the club. Failure to do so would bring severe repercussions from Hardaker's all-powerful Football League, resulting in a heavy fine or, even worse, the loss of points. After the near fiasco in Prague, Busby and club secretary Walter Crickmer vowed that this would never happen again and set in motion plans for better travel arrangements for future trips to Europe.

Busby, always looking for ways to improve the side, made a rare foray into the transfer market in December, when he signed the flamboyant and commanding goalkeeper Harry Gregg from Second Division Doncaster Rovers for £23,500 — at the time a world record fee for a goalkeeper. All that the Northern Ireland international received in the deal was £33 15s, his accrued share of benefit while with Doncaster. He turned out to be a bargain buy and is considered today to be the greatest United goalkeeper of all time. Gregg didn't have long to wait to make his debut.

On 21 December, just before the home match against Leicester City, Busby dropped five first-team regulars — goalkeeper Ray Wood, Jackie Blanchflower, Johnny Berry, David Pegg and Liam Whelan — all of whom had played a pivotal role in winning two League Championships. In their place he brought in Harry Gregg, Bobby Charlton, Mark Jones and Albert Scanlon.

Also making an appearance in the side was eighteen-year-old Welsh winger Kenny Morgans, an exciting all-round player who was enjoying a terrific run of form. Kenny had been spotted by Jimmy Murphy playing for Swansea Boys at Maine Road. Realising his great potential, he brought him to Old Trafford when he left school in the summer of 1955. Once selected for the first team he was never dropped, playing twenty-one games with every one won. Although he survived the air crash with superficial injuries and returned to play a handful of games for United, it was abundantly clear that he was a ghost of his former self, and he soon departed back to his native Wales with his full potential unexplored; another sad legacy of Munich.

All those players dropped by Busby at the end of 1957 were an integral part of the United squad and would at some point, if Munich hadn't intervened, have regained their places in the first team. Only Johnny Berry, who was over thirty, would have possibly struggled to oust the talented Kenny Morgans from his spot. The changes made by Busby had an immediate effect on the team's performance by thrashing Leicester 4–0, followed by a 3–0 home win on Christmas Day over Luton Town. The Babes, now back to their winning ways, soon began to close the gap with Wolves as they challenged for a third consecutive Championship.

The new year saw United embark on the FA Cup trail with a third-round tie against lowly Workington Town at Borough Park. Workington was managed by Joe Harvey, who had previously captained Newcastle United in the Wembley Cup finals of 1951 and 1952, and made it known he had scant regard for the reputation of Busby and his Babes. Although classed as an unfashionable Fourth Division side, they had in their line-up the big South African centre-forward Ted Purdon, who, according to Harry Gregg, 'liked to hurt goalkeepers for fun'. Two other exceptional players in the side were Bobby Mitchell and their record signing, Ken Chrisholme. They would prove to be no pushovers.

In front of 21,000 spectators packed into the tiny ground, Workington started strongly and in five minutes opened the scoring when Ted Purdon ran through the United defence unopposed. As Gregg raced out of his goal to intercept, Purdon at the last moment passed to Colbridge who slammed the ball into the empty net. From then on United struggled to find the form of a team that were odds-on favourite for the FA Cup and League Championship. It seemed the Fourth Division minnows were set for an unlikely giant-killing act.

On the half-time whistle the Workington players walked off to the cheers and applause of the exultant home fans. Although worthy of their one-goal lead, they should, on their performance, have been at least two up. In the United dressing room Busby gave the players one of his inspirational team talks. He urged Eddie Colman and Duncan Edwards to 'get Dennis on the ball'. With that United came out revitalised and, finding their feet, went to work mercilessly pressuring the Workington defence. The United players did exactly what Busby had instructed and got the ball to Dennis Viollet and in a six-minute spell he scored a pulverising hat-trick that turned the game around and saved United from a humiliating exit from the competition. Viollet's display of majestic ball control and balance showed why he was regarded by Busby as a striker of the highest order. From then on United clicked into gear and played like the champions they were, winning the game and progressing into the next round.

It was back to the League when United travelled to Leeds, coming away with a 1–1 draw, Dennis Viollet again the scorer. Three days later they faced Red Star Belgrade, another army team, in the first leg of the European Cup quarter-final at Old Trafford. Thick fog swirled around the ground, making playing conditions difficult for both teams. Although Charlton and Viollet came near to scoring in the opening minutes it was Belgrade's skilful inside-forward Tasic who netted first to put the visitors ahead.

Red Star's acrobatic goalkeeper Vladimir Beara, a former ballet dancer, in his all-black strip, deserved his nickname 'The Black Panther' as time after time he effortlessly kept the United strikers at bay. But United's persistent pressure paid off when Duncan Edwards passed the ball to Scanlon who centred for Bobby Charlton to bang it home. The players knew a draw wasn't good enough to take to Belgrade for the second leg; they needed to win the match, and dug deep to try and find something extra. They found it in Dennis Viollet. Racing in from the right wing he gracefully weaved his way through three Red Star defenders, leaving them flat footed, and swung the ball towards the goalmouth for Eddie Colman to score. United continued to pile on the pressure in the final ten minutes, searching for another goal, but were unable to find a way through. Referee Lesquenes blew his whistle to signal the end of an aggressive match with fouling from both sides. Although they had beaten Red Star 2–1, many felt that this slender one-goal advantage was not enough to see them through the second leg in Belgrade.

Four days later United focused their attention on the League title race when they faced a crucial fixture against Bolton Wanderers at Old Trafford on 18 January. Bolton were a formidable physical side, spearheaded by England international Nat Lofthouse with Roy Hartle and big John Higgins bolstering the defence, and not many First Division sides fancied their chances against them. Apart from their neighbours, Manchester City, Bolton was regarded by the United fans as the sworn enemy.

With United's steadily improving form the players were confident that they could overcome their bogey team and take both points from Bolton, and besides, they desperately wanted revenge for their 4–0 thrashing at Burnden Park earlier in the season. Their confidence was more than justified when they took Bolton by the scruff of the neck right from the start and played some devastating football that saw them win the game 7–2. The undoubted man of the match was the young blond-haired Bobby Charlton who scored a magnificent hat-trick. On-form Viollet put two away — his sixth goal since the New Year — with Albert Scanlon and Duncan Edwards adding to the tally with a goal apiece. United's savage demolition of Bolton Wanderers closed the gap to just six points behind top-of-the-table Wolves.

With this outstanding performance Busby knew his young team was just about as perfect as it could get. The introduction of wingers Kenny Morgans and Albert Scanlon had worked wonders, although it sidelined David Pegg and Johnny Berry. Pegg was not unduly worried about losing his place and was confident that in time he could win it back. However, Johnny Berry, who made his debut way back in 1951, was so distressed by his dropping that he put in a transfer request, but Busby, aware of his value to the club, turned him down point-blank.

A week later it was back to FA Cup action with a fourth-round tie against Second Division Ipswich Town. Little did the fans know that this was the last match the Babes would play at Old Trafford. Ipswich was managed at the time by Alf Ramsey, who famously went on to take England to World Cup victory in 1966. He had developed a talented side that had been promoted from the Third Division the previous season, thanks in the main to their prolific goal scorer Ted Phillips.

The 53,000 Old Trafford faithful saw Bobby Charlton continue his goal-scoring run with a pile-driving shot that gave the Ipswich goalkeeper Roy Bailey — father of Gary, a future United keeper — no chance of saving. With ten minutes left it was Charlton who sealed the game. Latching on to the ball, he threaded his way through the Ipswich defence to smack the ball into the roof of the net, putting United through to the next round against Sheffield Wednesday.

The Babes were flying high, progressing well on all fronts — the League, FA Cup and European Cup. The press and fans speculated that this was the season United would do the unimaginable — win the treble. If they did it would be an extraordinary achievement. But some football pundits wondered whether the strain of all these extra matches was taking its toll on the youngsters, and if they would, in striving for too many prizes, fail to last the course and end up grasping none.

Before United could prepare for the return leg against Red Star Belgrade there was the matter of an important League game against Arsenal at Highbury. Both clubs were known for their attacking style of play and the London press hyped up the game, predicting a classic encounter. The 63,000 capacity crowd that packed into the stadium was privileged to see one of the finest games ever played on an English football field and which is still referred to fifty years later as the 'The Great Match at Highbury'.

The team travelled down to London on the Friday and booked into the Lancaster Gate Hotel. The players were brimming with confidence and had the belief that they could beat anyone, but on the morning of the match their preparations were subdued when the 82-year-old club director George Whittaker was found dead in his hotel room. He had been a loyal and dedicated member of the club for over twenty years.

Captain Roger Byrne led out his team on to the field in their all-white Wembley strip, with black armbands as a mark of respect for their director. Busby kept with the same winning team for the sixth successive fixture: Gregg, Foulkes, Byrne, Colman, Jones, Edwards, Morgans, Charlton, Taylor, Viollet and Scanlon.

Arsenal were in the mid-table position and were a formidable side, especially on their home turf, with some outstanding players like the Welsh international goalkeeper Jack Kelsey, Dave Bowen, Derek Tapscott, Vic Groves and Jimmy Bloomfield. Also in the side was David Herd — Dennis Viollet's old schoolfriend, who went on to become a Scottish international and later enjoyed a distinguished career with Manchester United in the sixties.

As United warmed up on the pitch they were unaware that they were being watched by a small party of Yugoslav observers from the Red Star club, who had flown over to assess United's form before Wednesday's crucial quarter-final clash in Belgrade. What they witnessed that afternoon would give them deep cause for concern.

It was United's first trip to the capital that season and, as fate decreed, it would be their last. Never again would the Babes play on British soil and as if they sensed this they produced a most remarkable display of footballing brilliance. Right from the kick-off it was fluid end-to-end play from both teams but it didn't take long for United to get the upper hand with Morgans and Scanlon flying down their wings causing havoc. Inside ten minutes United were on the scoresheet, when Dennis Viollet dribbled his way through the Arsenal defence before picking out Kenny Morgans, who moved inside and rolled the ball to the oncoming Edwards. Although some twenty-five yards from the goal, Big Dunc didn't hesitate and blasted the ball through Jack Kelsey's hands into the corner of the net to open the scoring.

Arsenal fought back with the home fans cranking up the volume for all they were worth, urging them on. It took a superb save by Harry Gregg to keep the Gunners from equalising. His clearance was picked up by Albert Scanlon just inside his own half and he sprinted down the entire length of the left wing like a greyhound. Reaching the corner flag, he swung a perfect low pass to Bobby Charlton who smacked the ball home past a motionless Kelsey.

Arsenal, with the game slipping away, continued to push

forward in an attempt to salvage something. On one of their occasional excursions into the United half they thought they had pulled one back when Tapscott netted, but the linesman was in no doubt and flagged for offside, quickly silencing the premature celebrations of the home fans.

Three minutes before the interval it was Scanlon again who was the architect of United's third goal. He delivered a long accurate pass across field to Kenny Morgans on the opposite wing; Kenny, on seeing Tommy Taylor racing forward, rolled the ball into his path and watched 'The Smiling Executioner' cleanly dispatch the ball into the net to put United three up.

Much to Arsenal's relief the referee blew his whistle to signal half-time. The appreciative applause from the spectators reverberated around the stadium as both teams walked off the field for a well-deserved break. The fans knew they had witnessed a stunning display of footballing excellence; they had seen the Babes at their devastating best and waited in feverish anticipation for the second half to begin.

In the dressing room at half-time Roger Byrne gave his jubilant players, who were convinced the game was in the bag, a word of caution not to be complacent. 'This game is not over,' he warned. 'We are far too careless at the back.' His words proved to be prophetic.

During the interval Arsenal's manager, Jack Grayston, made some positional changes with Groves and Tapscott switching positions in the forward line. This arrangement seemed to have the desired effect, making the Arsenal attacking play more threatening.

Most teams trailing 3–0 against the Babes at their best would have been disheartened and rolled over, but Arsenal were having none of it — their pride was at stake. They came out for the second half and produced one of the finest displays of determination and character ever seen at the club.

Thirteen minutes into the second half they clawed their way back into the game with three goals scored in as many minutes. The first came about when their captain, Dave Bowen, rushed forward and delivered a long pass to David Herd, who coolly slipped the ball past Gregg. Two minutes later Nutt made a run down the left and crossed to Groves, who headed the ball down for Bloomfield to convert. Sensing they had United on the run, the Gunners piled on the pressure with Nutt repeating his left wing run, crossing to Bloomfield who headed the ball home past a startled Gregg. When Arsenal's third and equalising goal went in the mass of fans on the terraces went hysterical, shouting themselves hoarse. They knew they were witnessing a breathtaking display of football they would never forget.

United, their pride dented, still had the belief they could beat anyone. A cool Roger Byrne settled his players down while Duncan Edwards exhorted his teammates forward, and three minutes later United edged in front when Scanlon from the left linked up with Charlton who made a perfect pass for Viollet to score with a rare header.

Arsenal countered with numerous raids into the United half, with Groves, who had run tirelessly in midfield all afternoon, coming close, only to be denied by Harry Gregg. It was Gregg who initiated United's fifth goal in the seventy-first minute. After saving a ball from Herd's feet he cleared the ball up field to Kenny Morgans who swerved past an oncoming defender and sent a long pass out to Tommy Taylor. Tommy, running along the goal line with few options available in the middle, decided to shoot from an impossible angle, leaving Kelsey helpless.

Trailing 5–3 down with fourteen minutes left on the clock, Arsenal were not prepared to capitulate and pulled a goal back three minutes later to make it 5–4. The home fans exploded and roared the Gunners on to snatch a draw in the dying minutes. Fortunately the Babes hung on for the final whistle for a memorable and well-deserved victory. Both teams trooped off the muddy field to the thunderous applause from the appreciative crowd who felt privileged to have been part of something very special.

The only thing to mar United's celebrations was the news that Wolves had thrashed Leicester City 5–1 that afternoon, which pegged them at third spot in the table, six points behind the leaders. The players knew that when Billy Wright's Wolves visited Old Trafford the following Saturday it was going to be a crunch match that could, and probably would, decide the outcome of the Championship. But first they had the task of dispatching Red Star in Belgrade.

Chapter 6
End Game

After the shambles of trying to fly back from Prague after the Dukla game, the club directors were determined that this should never happen again. For the match against Red Star in Belgrade it was decided to charter their own aircraft for the exclusive use of the team, officials and press. British European Airways (BEA), who had carried the team on previous trips, were approached and duly laid on a 47-seat Airspeed Ambassador for their disposal.

BEA introduced the Ambassador in 1952 and assigned the class name 'Elizabethan' to the twenty aircraft in the fleet in honour of the newly crowned Queen. Compared with other aircraft around at the time its graceful design offered great passenger appeal. The high wing permitted an extremely quiet and spacious pressurised passenger cabin and offered unobstructed views from large panoramic windows. After a few annoying teething troubles were ironed out, BEA introduced the aircraft on most of its European routes, replacing its ageing Vickers Vikings and DC-3 Dakotas. However, the Elizabethan's reign was short lived due to the introduction of the turboprop Viscount in the mid fifties. In all only twenty-three aircraft were produced and after their retirement by BEA in 1958 the aircraft went on to enjoy a new lease of life with Dan Air London, flying holiday charters right up until 1971.

The pilot chosen to command the United flight was 36-year-old Captain James Thain. He first learned to fly, like many pilots of his generation, in the RAF during the war. After being demobilised from the Empire Air Navigation School in 1946 he went to Southampton University to study air navigation and after taking the appropriate examinations qualified for a commercial pilot's licence. He was accepted by BEA as a pilot on their formation in October 1946. He spent his first four years with the company as a first officer, bucketing around the skies of Europe in old twin-engined Vickers Vikings before attaining the rank of captain and transferring to the newly introduced Elizabethan. By 1958 he was classed as a senior captain with the airline and was also chairman of the Elizabethan panel in the British Airline Pilots' Association (BALPA), negotiating successfully with the BEA management on all matters relating to working conditions, schedules, routes and everything else concerning the Elizabethan operation. He was well liked by the colleagues he represented, so it came as no surprise when he received a phone call in January from the administrative officer offering him the special job of commanding the Belgrade flight.

Thain, who lived in Berkshire, had recently started up a poultry farming business in a nearby village, which he ran with the help of local labour. It was an interest that helped to occupy his time during the compulsory rest periods between flights. Poultry farming at the time had become a somewhat fashionable and popular hobby amongst airline pilots, and his close friend and colleague Captain Kenneth Rayment, who was also in the Elizabethan flight, expressed to Thain that he too was considering taking it up. It seems a strange paradox that both these men whose profession was flying should take up an interest in birds that cannot!

Rayment, who had been off duty for some time recovering from a hernia operation, had only recently returned to flying duties and that gave Thain an idea. He suggested to a helpful official in BEA that Rayment should be rostered on the Belgrade flight as his first officer. This, thought Thain, would give the two of them ample time on the four-day trip to discuss their mutual interest in greater detail. Thain had flown with Rayment before but on those occasions Thain's rank was first officer and he had flown under Rayment's command. Also included in the crew was George Rodgers, the radio officer; steward Tom Cable, a fervent United fan; and stewardesses Margaret Bellis and Rosemary Cheverton.

On Sunday 2 February the BEA Elizabethan G-ALZU, radio call sign Zulu Uniform, took off empty from London on a positioning flight to Ringway Airport, Manchester, where the aircraft remained overnight ready for an early start. The situation of two fully qualified captains on the flight deck was somewhat unusual, although not entirely unknown. Thain was the officially designated commander on the trip but, as was usual in these situations, he invited Rayment to share the flying. It was agreed between them that Thain would fly the outbound journey with Rayment acting as first officer and they would exchange roles on the return flight.

Rayment was slightly more senior than Thain in length of service and having more flying hours to his credit on Elizabethans. Like Thain, he had learned to fly in the RAF where he had a distinguished war record. He was Mentioned in Dispatches and awarded the DFC for his exploits, shooting down six enemy aircraft and a V1 flying bomb. In 1944 he was seconded to British Overseas Airways Corporation, based in Cairo, flying Lockheed Lodestars, and joined the newly-formed BEA in 1946. In March 1953 he completed a conversion course on the Elizabethan and had flown 3,143 hours on the type; his total flying hours amounted to an impressive 8,463.

It was a cold and grey miserable Monday morning when the United players and officials gathered at Old Trafford to catch the team coach to the airport. Mark Jones had to apologise to Matt Busby and endure some good-natured ribbing from his team-mates when he breathlessly arrived late. The only senior official of the club unable to make the trip was Jimmy Murphy who, in his other role as manager of the Welsh international side, was required in Cardiff for a World Cup qualifying game against Israel. Bert

Whalley, the team coach, stepped in at the last minute to take his place.

Back in 1958 Yugoslavia was seen as a secretive, hostile Communist country, so the wives, girlfriends and landladies made sure that the players were well prepared for their trip behind the 'Iron Curtain'. They packed sandwiches, hard-boiled eggs, biscuits, sweets and chocolate in fear of what awaited them on their arrival. Johnny Berry, so worried that he was going to starve, packed a Primus stove in his suitcase! In the event the food and service provided by the hotel was more than adequate.

Manchester in those days, like other industrial cities in the winter months, was subject to frequent fogs and smog caused by the belching polluting smoke churned out from the hundreds of factory chimneys, so it came as no surprise when the party arrived at Ringway to find the airport fog-bound and their flight delayed by over an hour. The players sat it out on basket chairs in the spartan surroundings of the departure lounge, joking, chatting and reading the match reports on their Arsenal game in the morning papers.

Players like Scanlon, Pegg, Colman and Foulkes enjoyed flying immensely while their captain, Roger Byrne, was a notoriously nervous flyer. Even Duncan Edwards, despite his evident interest in aviation shown by his frequent Sunday spotting trips to Ringway, was terrified. All of them were well aware of the inherent dangers in flying during that pioneering post-war period, for hardly a week went by without some air disaster being reported in the newspapers. And it must have been in all their minds that just eleven months earlier a BEA Viscount flying from Amsterdam had crashed into a row of council houses on the Ringway Airport boundary, killing all twenty on board plus two on the ground.

By eight o'clock the fog had lifted sufficiently for the party to board Zulu Uniform. The two stewardesses, Margaret Bellis and Rosemary Cheverton, stood by the cabin door welcoming everyone aboard, ticking off their names on the passenger list — a veritable who's who of footballing superstars. To Thain, who had no interest in football whatsoever, the names were meaningless, and he would be hard pressed, if asked, to even name their manager. Rayment, on the other hand, was well acquainted with most of the players, team officials and press, having been the pilot who flew them to and from Spain for their European Cup tie against Real Madrid the previous season.

Also travelling with the party to report on the game was a strong contingent of sports journalists representing the local and national press. Known to everyone as 'The Crazy Gang', they travelled thousands of miles each season to report on their exploits. Men like the genial pipe-smoking Alf Clarke from the now defunct *Manchester Evening Chronicle*, who was once on United's books even before Matt Busby arrived on the scene. He had reported on United for so many years that he showed not the slightest sign of impartiality in his match reports. Like a stick of Blackpool rock, he was Manchester United through and through. His close friend and rival, Tom Jackson from the *Manchester Evening News*, who had the ability to spew out match reports at breakneck speed from his typewriter, loved United with a passion and had reported on the team for over twenty-five years. The fans respected his writing and judgment and trusted him to tell them accurately about what was going on in the club. He was more than just a sports reporter — he was Manchester United's lifelong friend.

Reporters from the national newspapers included Donny Davies from the *Manchester Guardian*, as it was then known. He wrote a witty and widely read column under the pen name 'Old International', in which he brought football matches to life, especially when he was reporting on the Busby Babes. For most of his working life he was an education officer teaching young apprentices in a Manchester engineering company, but had secretly always had the ambition to be a sports writer. When the editor of the *Guardian* saw a fictitious match report he had written it was the beginning of a distinguished career in sports journalism.

The others who made up the press pack were: George Follows, *Daily Herald*; Archie Ledbrooke, *Daily Mirror*; Eric Thompson, *Daily Mail*; Henry Rose, *Daily Express*; and Frank Taylor, the chief sports reporter with the *News Chronicle and Daily Dispatch*, who survived the crash to read his own obituary printed by mistake.

Also travelling was Peter Howard, the *Daily Mail* photographer, and his telegraphist Ted Ellyard, who was responsible for wiring his pictures back home.

Finally there was the ever popular and irrepressible Frank Swift, known to all as 'Swifty', the gentle giant — a huge man with a huge sense of humour. He had made 209 consecutive appearances keeping goal for Manchester City and played in the same side with Matt Busby when City won the FA Cup in 1934. He made headlines that day when, overcome with emotion, he promptly fainted when the final whistle was blown, causing King George V to inquire how he was the following day. After he retired from the game he turned to sports writing and was on this trip reporting for the *News of the World*.

A direct flight to Belgrade was beyond the range of the Elizabethan so a refuelling stop was scheduled at Munich, which was accomplished with little difficulty. However, the second leg proved to be more troublesome. Belgrade was in the harsh grip of winter and the weather began to deteriorate as they approached the airport. But with some masterly piloting by Thain and Rayment they managed to touch down safely. Flying conditions were so dire that Zulu Uniform was the only aircraft that managed to land at Belgrade that day.

By teatime the team and officials had settled themselves in the Hotel Majestic in the city, where for some unknown reason armed guards patrolled every floor. Although sparse, the accommodation was comfortable and from the rear there were some stunning views over the River Danube. The hotel was only there, it appeared to the players, to impress foreign visitors. For the local population life was grindingly hard. Some of the players, out for a walk, could not help but notice the long queues at shops that contained precious little and were shocked to see people walking around in their bare feet despite the bitterly cold weather; the lucky ones shuffled about in shoes fashioned from old car tyres. Dennis Viollet remarked: 'We felt sorry for the people, especially the older ones and the children. If this is how communism was then they could keep it.' But it was not all gloom and doom; Tommy Taylor and Jackie Blanchflower, as usual up for some fun, found a frozen

Legends: The Busby Babes. Back row *left to right*: Matt Busby, Eddie Colman, Ray Wood, Mark Jones, Bill Foulkes, David Pegg, Duncan Edwards, Jimmy Murphy. Front row: Johnny Berry, Roger Byrne, Tommy Taylor, Dennis Viollet, Liam Whelan. (*Popperfoto/Alamy*)

Ready for departure: The British European Airways Elizabethan airliner — Zulu Uniform — being readied on the apron at a foggy Ringway Airport on Monday 3 February 1958. (*News group Newspapers Ltd*)

The last goodbye: The players, club officials and journalists pose for a press photograph before boarding the ill-fated Zulu Uniform. *Left to right*: standing in the entrance door Jackie Blanchflower, Bill Foulkes, Walter Crickmer, Donny Davies, Roger Byrne, Duncan Edwards, Albert Scanlon, the head of Frank Swift, Ray Wood, Dennis Viollet, Archie Ledbrooke, Geoff Bent, Mark Jones and Alf Clarke.

Scapegoat: Within hours of the crash the German authorities claimed that ice on the wings had caused the accident, thereby imputing the blame on Captain James Thain for not having his aircraft de-iced before departure. The conspiracy against him dragged on for eleven years before a British inquiry finally concluded that a build-up of slush on the runway was the cause of the accident. Harry Gregg says, 'Jim Thain was made a convenient scapegoat. It's time the real culprits, the men in the shadows, were finally dragged out to face the consequences. Just don't hold your breath.' (*Thain family archive*)

Fighter ace: A relaxed Captain Kenneth Rayment in BEA summer uniform outside his Glade Cottage home. Like many pilots of his generation he served in the RAF during the war and was awarded the DFC for shooting down six enemy aircraft and a V1 Flying Bomb. Critically injured in the accident he died in the Rechts der Isar Hospital the following month. (*Steve Rayment*)

Queen of the skies: The graceful lines of a BEA Elizabethan airliner in flight. (*Eddie Coates collection*)

Flying 1950s style: A rare interior photograph of Zulu Uniform taken in 1953 on its first visit to Ringway Airport. The high wing permitted an extremely quiet and roomy pressurised cabin with unobstructed views from large panoramic windows. Compared with other aircraft of the era, the Elizabethan's comfort and elegance of line drew great passenger approval. (*Les Jones*)

End game: The Babes line up for the final time in the Marakana Stadium before the game against Red Star Belgrade. Twenty-four hours later the team was decimated at Munich. *Left to right*: Duncan Edwards, Eddie Colman, Mark Jones, Kenny Morgans, Bobby Charlton, Dennis Viollet, Tommy Taylor, Bill Foulkes, Harry Gregg, Albert Scanlon and Captain Roger Byrne. (*Popperfoto/Alamy*)

Hero: United's flamboyant and commanding goalkeeper Harry Gregg was dubbed the hero of Munich. He ignored Captain Thain's warning to get clear and went back into the burning wreckage to help his teammates and rescue a young woman and her baby. (*Popperfoto/Alamy*)

Ablaze: The severed tail of Zulu Uniform burning fiercely in the oil compound. It was in this section that eight of Britain's top sports writers were killed.

Death of a queen: The forward section of the Elizabethan clearly showing where the tail section was completely severed aft of the wings. (*News group Newspapers Ltd*)

Otto Seffer

Karl-Heinz Seffer

Stewardess
Rosemary Cheverton

Ted Ellyard

Rescue: Father and son, Otto and Karl-Heinz Seffer astride the cockpit, work to free Captain Kenneth Rayment. (*Thain family archive*)

Devastation: The Elizabethan's starboard wing lies shattered in the snow. On the horizon the exploding oil compound sends billowing black smoke skywards.

lake nearby, and ignoring the risk of serious injury before such an important game went for a whirl on the ice. Luckily for them neither Busby nor any of the United officials caught them.

The following day the press pack, along with Captain Thain and his crew, went to the training ground to watch the players splash their way around the waterlogged track. Busby and team trainer Tom Curry kept a concerned eye on the injured Roger Byrne who was their only worry. But after going through his paces he signalled to his relieved manager that he was okay. With the Army Stadium where the match would be played close by, the team, after showering and changing, trooped off to inspect the playing conditions.

The evening before the game the players were taken to a nearby theatre to relax and wind down. Like everywhere else in Belgrade, armed guards patrolled the aisles and motioned to the locals in the first two rows to vacate their seats to make way for the United party. Much to the amusement of the players, one of the acts was a ham-fisted, incompetent magician. His performance was comical to say the least, with each and every trick going disastrously wrong. Although it was all good fun, the Babes couldn't wait for the show to end and head back to their hotel.

The day of the match dawned clear and sunny, and the hotel lobby was seething with excited football fans clamouring for autographs. No other international match had stirred up such massive interest. Soccer officials from all the Balkan countries as well as the European Cup Committee from Paris gathered in Belgrade to see the game and everywhere in the city there was a mad desperate scramble for tickets. The coach taking the players to the stadium passed thousands of chanting fans wending their way to the ground, who on catching sight of the team waved, smiled and roared: 'Busby Babes . . . Busby Babes . . . Busby Babes . . .'

The rising temperatures had thawed the pitch and, although frozen in parts with patches of snow, it was deemed playable. Roger Byrne remained in doubt right up to an hour before kick-off with Geoff Bent ready to step in if needed, but after a late fitness test the captain was finally declared fit — it was a close thing.

As the United players ran out of the tunnel into the warm afternoon sunshine they were met with the fearsome roar of 52,000 fervent partisan supporters including hundreds of khaki-clad conscripts who ringed the ground. There had been doubts in some quarters that United's 2–1 lead in the first leg at Old Trafford wouldn't be enough to see them through, but that idea quickly dissolved as the match got under way.

In a scintillating display of attacking football, United got off to a perfect start and inside two minutes they were a goal up, when a poor clearance by centre-half Spajic bounced off Tommy Taylor and went straight to Dennis Viollet, who seized on the rebound and gracefully steered the ball around the advancing goalkeeper to score. United could easily have been two up fourteen minutes later when Scanlon's corner, flicked on by Viollet, was hammered home by Bobby Charlton. But the Austrian referee, Karl Kainer, right up with play was in no doubt and disallowed it for offside.

But Charlton was not to be denied — after dispossessing Kostic as he tried to clear just outside the penalty area, he unleashed a thunderbolt of a shot towards goal. Beara, described at the time as the finest keeper in Europe, didn't stand a chance. Charlton, who was in fabulous form, was not finished yet. Two minutes later a free kick by Eddie Colman just outside the penalty area found Duncan Edwards, who uncharacteristically miskicked with the ball rolling to Charlton who picked his spot and smacked it home through a forest of defenders' legs to put United three up, silencing the hostile crowd.

Red Star were rocked by the onslaught and tempers became frayed. Kenny Morgans had his right thigh ripped open by an over-zealous tackle but the referee was totally blind to the blatant foul. The game raged on and United's brilliant display of teamwork completely outfoxed and subdued the Yugoslavs. The only thing to spoil the flow of play was the frequent whistle-blowing from Kainer, mainly against the United tackles, which would have been considered more than fair in England. Eric Thompson of the *Daily Mail* felt that the referee 'would have been howled off an English ground for his niggling, anti-tackling phobia' and Henry Rose of the *Daily Express* wrote in his match report, 'I thought Herr Kainer would have given a free kick against United when one of the ball boys fell on his backside!' Almost on the stroke of half-time, with the United forwards still probing and pushing forward, Duncan Edwards hit a blistering shot that was saved by Beara, almost carrying him over the goal line with its ferocity. So powerful was the drive that it burst the ball, leaving Kainer to signal the bench for a replacement.

When the half-time whistle blew United trotted off the pitch 3–0 up, but it could easily have been four or five. As at Highbury the previous Saturday, when United seemed to have the game in the bag by half-time, they had again allowed an apparently beaten team to stage an unlikely comeback — they had obviously learned little from their London experience.

No doubt after a tough half-time team talk by their manager, Red Star came out for the second half very much fired-up and, roared on by the home crowd, pulled out everything to save the match. Within two minutes Kostic, after appearing to obstruct Eddie Colman, ran through and fired off a twenty-yard shot that just evaded Gregg's grasping fingers to pull a goal back. The home crowd went into frenzy and Red Star, their confidence and self-respect restored, launched wave after wave of attacks on the United goal.

With their backs to the wall the Babes thought they were playing against twelve men, with the referee giving every decision to the home side. What happened next only served to underline it. Bill Foulkes challenged Tasic for possession in the United penalty area; Tasic seemingly lost his balance and fell to the floor, pulling Foulkes down on top of him. It was a dubious foul at best but Kainer had no hesitation in giving the penalty. Roared on by the crowd, Tasic converted from the spot to make it 3–2. The home supporters broke into an uncontrolled frenzy of jubilation and excitement. Pushing forward to get a better view of the action, a seething mass of fans came tumbling down the terraces, overflowing onto the pitch behind Gregg's goal.

Red Star's furious pace never slackened. As the Babes tried to find their flowing, attacking play of the first half, they were pelted by a storm of snowballs from the hostile crowd. On their occasional counter-attacks United still looked dangerous, and on one breakaway Kenny Morgans was unlucky when his shot ricocheted off the post with the keeper beaten. Then, with just two minutes to go before the final whistle, Harry Gregg raced out of his goal and threw himself full length at the feet of the advancing Tasic. He grasped the ball cleanly, but the impetus of his dive took him outside the penalty area. Kostic took the resulting free kick from twenty-five yards out and fortuitously for Red Star and unluckily for United the ball was deflected off Dennis Viollet's head, sending Gregg the wrong way and the ball into the net. It was now 3–3 and Red Star desperately wanted win the game, but United kept their heads and somehow managed to hold on. If they thought the barrage from the fans was over when the final whistle blew, they were mistaken; as the Babes trooped off the pitch the home crowd again pelted them with snowballs!

The match, particularly the second half, had been intemperate and coloured by some extraordinary and, from United's point of view, bizarre refereeing from Karl Kainer. During the match he awarded twenty-four free kicks against United and just eleven against Red Star, not to mention the hotly disputed penalty against Foulkes. His inept handling of the game was criticised in all the English match reports.

Forty years later, two television researchers tracked down the referee to his home in Austria to interview him for a documentary. Kainer, then in his eighties, told them, 'I can't remember a game, in all the 1,812 games I've refereed, where I got such a bad press.' During the interview the researchers also discovered the location of the ball from that final game. The original match ball which burst — not surprisingly after one of Duncan Edwards's blistering shots — was replaced, and eventually found its way into Kainer's trophy cabinet. He told them, 'Balls are my weakness. I love balls as souvenirs, all my concentration and thoughts were focused during the game on taking the ball home with me.' To this end, Kainer put into operation his highly refined ball entrapment technique. 'I always carry a net around with me in my suitcase and I hang the net around inside my overcoat with the ball in it. And it has always worked. I have managed to bring home about twenty balls from really big, important games in Italy, and these balls now reside in my cabinet at home.'

It was a very much relieved Roger Byrne who led his team off the field. It had been a close run thing, but all that mattered now was they were through to the semi-finals of the European Cup for the second consecutive season. Busby called it 'as great a performance as I have ever seen from our lads'. In the dressing room they were joined by the press pack and Jim Thain and his crew to celebrate with bottles of beer brought over from Manchester by Bert Whalley and Tom Curry; the stewardesses discreetly waited outside until the players had showered and changed. Meanwhile Busby, being the diplomat that he was, sportingly went to the Red Star dressing room to thank them for a good game.

With the trials and tribulations over it was now time to relax, celebrate and enjoy the post-match banquet at the hotel in Belgrade where they were joined by their opposite team members from Red Star. In those early days of the European Cup there was a great camaraderie between clubs and despite the disappointment felt by the host club it turned out to be a jovial and friendly affair.

The banquet room was opulent, and as if to demonstrate the dominance of Communism a shining silver replica of the Russian earth-orbiting sputnik satellite circled the room on rails as violinists played. All this of course was show for the benefit of foreign visitors and didn't delude anyone about the hardship and suffering experienced by ordinary Yugoslavian people.

As the long speeches came to an end, the three Yorkshire players — Tommy Taylor, David Pegg and Mark Jones — gave a rendition of their native anthem, 'On Ilkley Moor Baht hat', with the rest of the team joining in. With the pressure off and sleep out of the question the lads wanted to go out on the town. As the proceedings drew to a close Roger Byrne passed a note down the table to Matt Busby asking if they could leave early and go out for a few drinks. Busby read the note, puffed on his pipe and smiled, 'Just half an hour.' There was a chorus of protests from the players and after further consideration Busby agreed to an extra half-hour.

Roger Byrne and a number of the players drifted off to the British Embassy Staff Club where they spent the rest of the night drinking and dancing. With Busby's one o'clock curfew drawing near, a BEA representative along with an Embassy staff member drove Roger and Mark Jones back to their hotel. But still in the mood to party, they made a quick exit out of a rear window without being noticed and climbed back into the car to be whisked off to the home of a Canadian couple where the celebrations continued well into the early hours. It was past three in the morning when Roger and Mark crept silently back into the hotel hoping not to be discovered.

The rest of the players decided to shun the bright lights and fleshpots of downtown Belgrade and returned to the hotel. Harry Gregg recalled: 'We played poker into the wee small hours, with me betting sterling and the rest of the lads extortionate amounts of the near-worthless local currency. "I'll see you four grand!" Boy, did they think they were high rollers. Despite the fact that I was putting in ten-shilling notes, whilst the other lads threw down Yugoslav currency and lifted mine, I still managed to skin the school. We also opened the suitcases full of food we'd been advised to bring from home, tucking into an eclectic, and late night, gastronomic feast which included corned beef, hard-boiled eggs and biscuits.'

That night of celebrations at the hotel is clearly remembered by one of Yugoslavia's most renowned journalists Miroslav (Miro) Radojcic. In his article for his newspaper *Politika*, he wrote: 'Then followed the simple warm-hearted words of Matt Busby and Walter Crickmer as they said, "Come and visit us, the doors of Old Trafford will always be open to you."' Donny Davies from the *Manchester Guardian* said to Radojcic as he left the banquet, 'Why didn't you score just one more goal, then we could have met for a third time in the replay.'

After spending some time after the party chatting and drinking with Tommy Taylor and Duncan Edwards in a local bar, Radojcic went back to his office and wrote up his piece for the paper, then sat up for most of the night musing about a feature article that he planned to write about Manchester United. Suddenly, the idea occurred to him to write his story from the Manchester viewpoint, and there and then he decided to fly back to Manchester with the players. He went back to his flat, quickly packed a bag and set off for the airport, only to find on arrival he had left his passport behind. He pleaded with the airport authorities to hold the aircraft for as long as possible while he returned home. By the time he got back the apron was deserted. Later when he heard the shocking news of the disaster he could only wonder . . . what if.

Chapter 7
Prelude to Disaster

The next morning there were some sore and tired heads amongst the jubilant United party when they said their farewells to the hotel staff and boarded the coach to Belgrade's Zemun Airport for the flight home. In addition to the group that had flown out from Manchester three days earlier, an extra five people had now been added to the passenger list: Verena Lukic, wife of the Yugoslav air attaché in London and her baby daughter; travel agent Bela Miklos and his wife, Maria, who had arranged the trip; and Yugoslav diplomat Nebosja Tomasevich. This brought the total number boarding the aircraft to thirty-eight. But with the Elizabethan's 47-seat capacity there was still plenty of room for everyone to seat themselves comfortably wherever they liked in the cabin.

There were ten rows of seats, of which the four nearest the cockpit faced the rear and the remaining six faced forward. Peter Howard and his assistant, Ted Ellyard, settled themselves in the far right-hand corner behind the forward bulkhead which separated the cabin from the cockpit. In the row in front of them sat the United goalkeeper Harry Gregg.

Frank Taylor of the *News Chronicle*, on a hunch, also decided to sit up front; he positioned himself on the left-hand side, three rows back from the bulkhead in a rearward facing seat, rather than with his press friends in the tail. 'It was just a silly whim,' he said. 'Last night in Belgrade, after the banquet, a combination of clammy central heating, the food, and perhaps the high-pressure worries of getting the story back to England, had knocked me for six. On a previous flight from Prague we'd been bunched up in the tail and it was just a wee bit bumpy flying over the Alps. I didn't fancy a recurrence of that sinking feeling, so I moved forward to that rearward facing seat.'

On the flight deck seating arrangements were also being discussed. Since Thain had flown the two legs of the outbound flight to Belgrade, it had been agreed that Rayment would operate the return journey, and that posed a small, but in the light of what was to happen in the next few hours, significant problem.

A BEA staff instruction, introduced in 1956, firmly stated that the pilot in command (in this instance Thain) must always occupy the cockpit's left-hand seat, even if he was not actually the pilot flying the aircraft — but if Thain was to now act as co-pilot he really needed to be in the right-hand seat, where it was easier to see certain vital instruments and gauges which had to be monitored during the critical stages of landing and take-off.

This was not a new problem and it occurred frequently when pilots exchanged control on long flights. As a general rule, BEA pilots would unofficially swap seats, breaching company regulations in doing so but making it easier and safer for the first officer to become 'pilot in charge'. So this is what Thain and Rayment agreed to do on that cold Thursday morning at Belgrade Airport.

It made perfect sense, after all Rayment was an experienced captain in his own right and had more flying hours in charge of the Elizabethan than Thain; he was perfectly used to being in the left-hand seat and handling the flying controls from that position. Although sitting there contravened a company staff instruction, he was in reality only following 'current unofficial practice' among BEA pilots. It was a decision that was soon to have far-reaching consequences for both of them.

Before departure there had been a lengthy delay owing to some confusion over Johnny Berry's passport and visa. It was as if the Yugoslav authorities were determined to hang on to the little outside-right for themselves. Eventually, after an intensive search, his documents were located onboard the aircraft and when everything was sorted out to the satisfaction of the airport officials the party were allowed on their way.

It was late in the morning when Zulu Uniform finally took off from Belgrade in intermittent sunshine and snow showers. Ominously, the onward forecast for Munich, the refuelling stop, was dire, with low cloud down to 500 feet, driving rain and snow. In the cabin the players settled down for the three-hour flight, passing the time as best as they could playing cards, reading, chatting and sleeping off their hangovers, while in the tail the pressmen swapped stories and angled for scoops.

Across the aisle from Frank Taylor, within touching distance, Harry Gregg lay curled up across two seats, catching up on much-needed sleep. Yesterday in Belgrade Gregg was the man of action, frantically leaping about his goal to thwart Red Star's fierce second-half onslaught, and so helping United hang on for a place in the semi-finals. Even when the excited home fans tumbled down the terraces and surged onto the pitch behind the goalmouth his eyes never left the ball. It was probably Gregg's greatest game since signing for the club. In fact United had remained unbeaten since his debut against Leicester City in December.

In front of Gregg, Bill Foulkes was engrossed in a four-handed game of hearts with David Pegg, Albert Scanlon and Kenny Morgans. Across the aisle, at a six-seater table, another card school was underway, with Liam Whelan, Johnny Berry, Roger Byrne, Ray Wood and Jackie Blanchflower all staking a claim for top spot at poker.

Behind them, Frank Taylor passed his time gazing out of the cabin window at the inhospitable scenery below. With a BEA route map in hand he tried with little success to identify the jagged snow-covered mountain ranges that slowly slipped by beneath the aircraft. Then, tired of his self-imposed isolation, he decided to move down the cabin to join his jovial press friends in the tail. Passing by the card schools he momentarily paused as he came abreast of Matt Busby who looked tired and grey-faced. Just three weeks earlier he had slipped quietly into a Manchester hospital for an operation and now this 2,000-mile round trip was taking its toll. Busby felt his boys needed him and was determined to be with them for this crucial game. Now, thought Taylor as he sat down next to his colleagues, the United manager was paying the price for his dedication.

Time quickly passed in the warm confines of the insulated cabin, filled with the chatter of the pressmen and players and the laughter and cries of frustration from the card players. A low chime sounded on the cabin intercom and a stewardess informed the passengers to fasten their seat belts and extinguish their cigarettes as the aircraft was about to land at Munich, where they would be given light refreshments while the aircraft was refuelled.

In the cockpit there was no time for relaxation as Rayment and Thain began their descent towards Munich through 18,000 feet of solid cloud. With an outside temperature plummeting to minus 21 degrees centigrade, they switched on the airframe anti-icing equipment. This system heated air to 60 degrees centigrade by fuel burners in the wings, vented under pressure through ducting to the leading edges of the wings, tail plane and fins to prevent the formation of ice, which could seriously affect the flying characteristics of the aircraft.

Zulu Uniform slithered through the overcast at 500 feet into something approaching a blizzard. The runway was just discernible against a vast expanse of white by black streaks made by departing and landing aircraft. It was a tricky approach for the crew in the driving snow and called for some skilful flying. The touchdown was normal, but as the Elizabethan rolled down the runway great bow-waves of brown slush were thrown up from the wheels, giving the passengers the feeling they were touching down in the sea. The drizzle, which had been falling throughout the morning at Munich, had now turned to snow, leaving a jellified watery mass on the apron through which Rayment taxied the aircraft to a halt in front of the terminal building. The time was just after 13.15 hours GMT (14.15 hours local). Zulu Uniform would never fly again.

Munich, the capital of Bavaria, that day looked cold, grey and inhospitable like some far-flung Siberian outpost. For a few of those on board, with the war still fresh in their minds, it brought back memories that this was the infamous city which gave birth to the Nazi movement; the city that Neville Chamberlain flew to in 1938 to negotiate the Munich Settlement with Hitler and the subsequent shame of 'Peace for our time!'

Although much of the city had been pounded by bomber command during the war it had recovered remarkably quickly and still had some compelling attractions such as its famous art gallery, theatres, and — perhaps of more interest to the players — the beer cellars! But with the refuelling stop scheduled for just an hour there would be no time for sightseeing.

When the door opened, a bitterly cold blast of air entered the warm cabin. The passengers clattered down the steps and scurried across the treacherous tarmac in the swirling snow for the shelter of the airport lounge and the promise of hot drinks and refreshments. On the way David Pegg and Eddie Colman, always ready for some fun, pelted the ground crew with snowballs, then quickly ran into the terminal before they had the chance to return fire. Inside it was pleasantly warm, with the usual tables and chairs scattered about and the walls adorned with travel posters and route maps. Large panoramic windows ran the entire length of the room, giving everyone an uninterrupted view of the wintry scene outside. Some of the players gathered around the counter of a little gift shop in the corner to buy last minute presents for family and friends back home, while the press pack gathered in a small annex to the main lounge and chatted about the annual Manchester Press Ball due to take place that evening.

As Maria Miklos, wife of the travel courier, went from table to table making sure that everyone had sandwiches and a hot drink, the door suddenly opened letting in an icy blast of air. It was latecomer Roger Byrne, holding the door open far longer than was necessary. With howls of protest from his fellow players, Byrne grinned, 'What's the matter, someone cold?' The Babes' captain, a keep-fit fanatic, despised the wearing of an overcoat even in the depths of winter, preferring to walk about with no more protection than his United blazer. Snuggled deep in his armchair, Duncan Edwards yelled at him, 'For Pete's sake, Rog, shut the ruddy door.' Other players broke into a rendition of 'Baby it's cold outside . . .' and even Matt Busby managed a weak smile at his boy's antics.

Meanwhile, Thain and Rayment left the aircraft and walked over to the Meteorological office to get the onward weather forecast, leaving Bill Black, the BEA station engineer, to supervise the refuelling. As the only licensed Elizabethan engineer on duty at the airport he could not, for technical reasons, use the under-wing pressurised system to refuel and so, aided by the local ground staff, had to resort to using the emergency fillers on top of the wings. Although it was still snowing, the wings were still warm from the de-icing applied during the descent and any flakes falling on the wings melted on contact, the resulting water draining away from the trailing edge. As Bill Black walked along the wing during the refuelling operation he noticed no snow or ice adhering to the wings and had no difficulty maintaining his footing.

After completing the departure details in the Met office, Thain took the paperwork to Air Traffic Control while Rayment went to the BEA office. Meeting up outside, they walked slowly back to the aircraft and discussed the amount of snow that had fallen on the wings. 'I studied the snowfall on the starboard wing,' recalls Thain. 'I had to wait until I got fairly close before I could really identify any snow, and when I got close I saw a thin film of partially melted snow on the wing. It had thawed in places and I could see the water from the melted snow running off the trailing edge right along the wing.' Rayment expressed the opinion that it was not necessary to have the wings swept and de-iced; Thain agreed and then went to the BEA office to have the ship's papers signed. Bill Black, after completing his pre-departure inspection of the aircraft, approached Thain and asked him if he should have the aircraft de-iced. Thain told him that it was not necessary. Other aircraft departing Munich that day all had de-icing undertaken, more as a matter of routine than anything else; with the temperature just above freezing it simply was not required.

When Zulu Uniform landed at Munich there were two minor items entered in the technical log: the toilet pump was unserviceable, and the fresh water tank in the galley required topping up. Bill Black issued instructions to the ground crew for these defects to be attended to. As Thain was about to enter the aircraft, he noticed one of the airport workers struggling to lift a heavy hose up to the servicing panel, just aft of the crew door, to replenish the water tank. Unlike Black when he had stood on the wing, he couldn't keep his grip on the slippery surface of the apron. Thain went over to help, planting a foot firmly behind the man's heel to help him get the purchase he needed to connect up the hose. During the filling operation, which lasted three or four minutes, Thain stood between the fuselage and the starboard engine, all the time watching the thawing snow drip off the trailing edge of the wing. It convinced him that he was right in his decision not to have the aircraft de-iced.

Soon the passengers were traipsing back to the aircraft, clutching their bags of duty-free and presents for family and friends back home. They settled into their seats, in much the same positions as at the start of the previous leg of the journey, and at 14.20 hours (15.20 hours local), a little over one hour after arrival, Zulu Uniform was ready to depart.

Zulu Uniform: *Munich tower, B-line 609 Zulu Uniform, taxi clearance please.*
Tower: *609 Zulu Uniform, Munchen tower, wind two nine zero, eight knots. Cleared to runway two five. QNH one zero zero four, time one nine and a quarter, over.*
Zulu Uniform: *Roger, thank you.*

Both Thain and Rayment knew that the runway was covered with a layer of slush, but with the knowledge at the time did not consider it excessive, especially since the first two thirds of the runway were well trodden by previous aircraft landing and taking off. A few minutes later Zulu Uniform approached the threshold and was cleared to enter the runway.

Tower: *B-line 609, cleared to line up and hold, and here is your clearance, over.*

Zulu Uniform: *609, understand, I am cleared to line up and hold. I am ready for the clearance.*

Tower: *Munich control clears B-line 609 Zulu Uniform to the Manchester airport via amber airway one zero, green airway one, amber two, amber one and route as filed. Maintain one seven thousand feet. Right turn after take-off. Climb on south course inbound to the Friesing range, over.*

Zulu Uniform repeated the clearance back to the tower. With the Elizabethan lined up with the runway centre line and the brakes confirmed set, the throttle levers, which were mounted on a pedestal between the two pilots, were opened up for a final power check before departure.

Tower: *B-line 609, how long will it take for the engine run, over?*
Zulu Uniform: *Half a minute.*
Tower: *Ah, roger. Your clearance expires at three one. Time now three zero.*

With just a minute left before their clearance expired, the pilots quickly concluded the engine run and with all cockpit checks completed they were ready to depart.

Zulu Uniform: *Ah, Munich, 609 Zulu Uniform, I am ready for take-off.*
Tower: *609 Zulu Uniform, wind two nine zero, one zero knots, cleared for take-off, right turn out.*
Zulu Uniform: *Thank you.*

Rayment, from the left-hand seat, slowly advanced the throttles with his right hand and Thain, as procedure demanded, followed through with his left. Zulu Uniform began to roll down the runway, gradually gathering speed, with the nosewheel creating a great bow-wave of slush. When the throttles were fully forward against the stops, Thain rapped the back of Rayment's hand for him to relinquish control. Rayment then called out, 'Check full power.' Thain confirmed, 'Full power set, temperatures and pressures OK, warning lights out.' As the aircraft barrelled down the runway Thain called out the increasing speeds in knots. Suddenly both pilots heard an uneven note in the port engine. Thain quickly scanned the instruments and caught sight of a fluctuating pressure gauge. At the same time Rayment shouted 'Abandon take-off' and with his right hand slammed the throttles shut, catching Thain's knuckles in the process. The brakes were applied and Zulu Uniform shuddered to a halt half-way down the runway.

> Zulu Uniform: *609, we are abandoning the take-off.*
> Tower: *Say again please.*
> Zulu Uniform: *We are abandoning the take-off. May we backtrack, over?*
> Tower: *609, cleared to backtrack.*
> Zulu Uniform: *Thank you.*

As Thain blew on the back of his grazed hand Rayment apologised, having little need to explain that the emergency required prompt action. The problem with the port engine was a familiar one known as boost surging, a fault that had plagued the Elizabethan since its introduction into BEA service in 1952. It was caused in the main by an over-rich fuel mixture creating uneven engine running and was more acute in thin air at high altitude airports such as Munich, which lay just north of the Alps at an elevation of more than 1,700 feet.

In the passenger cabin, as the aircraft violently came to a stop, Tommy Cable, the white-jacketed steward, came clattering out of the forward galley and was pitched into the rearward facing seat next to Verena Lukic and her baby daughter. White-faced and visibly shaken, he quickly strapped himself into the seat beside them. Somehow he had been stranded in the galley on take-off when he should have been seated in the tail. There was no discernible panic amongst the rest of passengers, just frowns and puzzled looks and the inevitable question, Why hadn't the plane taken off?

Zulu Uniform turned around and taxied back down the runway through the rutted slush to the threshold for a second attempt. As

Thain and Rayment discussed the surging problem they were interrupted by a call from the tower.

> Tower: *609, for your information, we have a car on the runway which will be removed any second.*
> Zulu Uniform: *Have car on the runway?*
> Tower: *Disregard. The car is leaving the runway now . . . it's at the other end.*

On the flight deck, the deliberation continued. The pilots knew that the boost surging should not theoretically cause much reduction in overall take-off power, but because of the uneven engine note it gave the impression of poor engine performance, and no pilot worth his salt would be willing to take off if he thought the engines were not up to scratch. They both knew that boost surging could be caused by, among other things, opening the throttles too quickly. Rayment told Thain that on the next take-off attempt he would open the throttles a little before releasing the brakes and then continue to open them up more slowly until full power was achieved. This was the accepted corrective action and had been successfully used before in such circumstances.

Zulu Uniform, approaching the runway threshold, requested clearance for take-off:

> Zulu Uniform: *Munich from 609 Zulu Uniform. When we get to the end of runway we should like to take-off again. Is the clearance still valid?*
> Tower: *609, your clearance is still valid. However, maintain five thousand feet until further advised. The wind three zero zero, eight knots, cleared for take-off.*
> Zulu Uniform: *Thank you. Understand, maintain five thousand feet until further advised.*

Again Thain and Rayment went through the departure checks and lined the aircraft up with the runway centre line. With the brakes set, the throttles were opened up to 28 inches of boost. The brakes were released and Zulu Uniform rolled forward, gathering speed on its second take-off run. This time Rayment eased the throttles gently forward with Thain following through. He then requested 'full power check'. Thain scanned the engine instruments and confirmed the settings. 'Full power ch . . . ' Before he could complete the sentence the needle of the port engine pressure gauge shot off the clock.

'Abandon take-off!' This time it was Thain who had made the decision to abort. The throttles were slammed back and full braking applied. Forty seconds after the take-off commenced the aircraft slowed to taxi speed halfway down the runway. Evidently the recommended procedures hadn't worked and Thain decided to return to the terminal for further consultation with the BEA engineer.

Zulu Uniform: *Munich, 609 Zulu Uniform, we are abandoning this take-off as well.*
Tower: *Ah, roger, cleared to backtrack.*
Zulu Uniform: *We would like to be cleared back to the tarmac, over.*
Tower: *Roger, cleared to the ramp.*
Zulu Uniform: *Understand, cleared to backtrack and cleared to the tarmac.*
Tower: *You are cleared to backtrack or cleared to taxi via crosswing as desired.*
Tower: *B-line 609, do you wish to make another take-off right now or do you wish to wait at the ramp? Over.*
Zulu Uniform: *609 Zulu Uniform, I am returning to the tarmac. I am returning to the tarmac — to the terminal, over.*
Tower: *Roger, that is understood.*

In the cabin the passengers sat back in consternation. Bill Foulkes felt uneasy and thought there was something not quite right with the aircraft. Two rows behind, Ted Ellyard glanced out of his window and joked that the engine looked as though it could have done with a little bit more elastic. But in the tail a concerned Frank Swift leapt to his feet and roared, 'What the bloody hell is going on here?'

On clearing the runway Thain took control and had some difficulty in following the taxiway lines, which were now almost obliterated in the fresh fall of snow. Meanwhile Rayment, for the first time, made an announcement to reassure his bewildered and nervy passengers. He explained that a technical fault had prevented their departure and they were returning to the terminal for further checks. Rayment then resumed control and brought the aircraft to a halt in front of the terminal, exactly twenty minutes since they had first departed.

The prospect of the United team getting home that day was rapidly receding.

Chapter 8
Runway

As the cabin door opened it was a somewhat sombre party that trooped down the aircraft steps for the second time and trudged through the glutinous slush back to the warmth of the terminal building. After two aborted take offs the atmosphere amongst them was decidedly tense. Questions were now being tossed about between them as to why they had not taken off. Journalist Frank Taylor, who had served in the RAF during the war, thought that ice on the wings had possibly caused the failure to get airborne. 'With those thoughts racing through my mind,' he said, 'I looked hard at the high wing of the Elizabethan. But it was impossible from the ground to get a full view of the upper surfaces. But why was I concerned? The ground crew, when they refuelled, would have checked that, and it was thirteen years since I had last serviced a plane; they would know what they were doing. So I swept those idle thoughts from my mind and entered into the fug and fun in the lounge.'

Once assembled inside the terminal any nervousness quickly dissolved as the party indulged in the inevitable round of joking and tomfoolery. Big Frank Swift, over 6 feet tall, weighing 14 stone and with an even bigger sense of humour, swapped overcoats with the small rotund pressman Eric Thompson. Eric shuffled around the room with the coat trailing the floor, to everyone's amusement, while Frank tried to cram his massive frame into Eric's. 'Must have shrunk,' he said, grinning.

As Maria Miklos, wife of the travel courier, dashed about making sure everyone had a hot drink, some of those present felt that they wouldn't be flying home that afternoon. Duncan Edwards immediately rushed off a telegram to his landlady in Manchester: 'All flights cancelled returning home tomorrow'. Alf Clarke from the *Evening Chronicle,* anxious to get back to Manchester for that evening's Press Ball, where Frank Swift was to be MC, hurried off to telephone a short story about the hold-up to his paper. Even Matt Busby was heard to say in conversation that if it wasn't so important to get the lads back to Manchester for a good night's sleep before Saturday's game, they could return tomorrow morning.

As soon as the passengers had disembarked, Bill Black, the station engineer, clattered up the steps and entered the flight deck to find out why they had returned to the ramp. What was discussed between them in the next five minutes would decide the fate of Flight 609.

Thain explained to him about the boost surging in the port engine on the two previous take-off attempts. Black agreed that it was a common problem with the Elizabethan when operating at high altitude airports, and that if the recommended procedures of opening the throttles slowly had failed then the only other solution was to have the engines retuned, a lengthy procedure that would mean an overnight stop.

Thain, anxious to stay on schedule, thought that this seemed a bit drastic and suggested that if the throttles were opened up even more slowly then there was a good chance of solving the problem. This would mean the take-off speed being reached further down the runway. But with 1,908 metres available to the aircraft, this should not pose a problem. After further consultation with Rayment, Thain, as aircraft commander, made the decision that they would try for a third attempt. Realising that the passengers had been offloaded, he instructed Black to put out the call to the traffic officer to summon them back to the aircraft.

However, the question of whether to de-ice the aircraft before departure had to be decided again. Thain later said: 'I talked to Captain Rayment about the snow. We both looked out of our respective windows and studied our respective wings and we found that we had lost that very thin film of partially melted snow which I had observed walking out to the aircraft, and from my seat the wing appeared quite clean. I again considered that there was no necessity to have the wings swept.' Bill Black walked around the aircraft during this period but saw nothing amiss. Thain's decision not to de-ice the aircraft was to haunt him for the next eleven years.

The condition of the runway, however, was far from satisfactory. There had been no attempt made by the airport authority to sweep the runway clear of snow and slush. Ominously, very little was known in the 1950s regarding slush and its effects on aircraft performance. The Canadians had undertaken some research and it was known as a hazard and cause for concern, but no one had done the vital research necessary to obtain a better understanding of its effects and warn airport authorities and airlines of its potential danger. The BEA flight manuals contained virtually no information for pilots attempting to take off from contaminated runways and the decision, rightly or wrongly, was left entirely to the aircraft commander.

After two abandoned take-offs, Zulu Uniform had now become the centre of attention and a number of people were watching the departure preparations with great interest.

In his first floor office Count Rudolph zu Castell, the airport director, waiting for the expected arrival of Chancellor Erhardt later that afternoon, looked down from his window at the bleak wintry scene below. On the floor above, a group of trainees from the Air Navigation School stood by the windows watching the activity around the aircraft, thought they detected a thin layer of snow on the wings and wondered why it hadn't been swept clean. One even took a photograph — a photograph that would become the subject of a great deal of controversy in the years to come. A German army officer and his companion, on a tour of the airport, who had watched the first two abandoned take-off attempts from the control tower, now took up a strategic position on the apron and waited patiently for the aircraft to taxi out. Zulu Uniform, it seemed, would not be allowed to depart Munich that afternoon unobserved.

For the second time that day the airport Volkswagen, carrying two airport workers, was dispatched to carry out another survey of the runway in preparation for the arrival of the German Chancellor. The inspection was cursory at best, stopping in only a few places to measure the depth of slush. The survey completed, they reported about one centimetre of slush over the entire length of the runway. Other pilots landing at Munich that day reported that many areas were much deeper with large pools of standing water. The first two thirds of the runway were well rutted with tyre tracks from arriving and departing aircraft, but the last third was covered with an even layer of undisturbed wet slush.

Over the tannoy in the airport lounge came a disembodied German voice summoning the waiting passengers to board the aircraft. Everyone was taken by surprise since less than ten minutes had elapsed since they had disembarked — surely they couldn't have fixed the fault in such a short time? With half-drunk cups of coffee pushed aside, the chairs scraped the floor as everyone stood up and made for the exit. Tom Curry, the United trainer, positioned himself by the door to count everyone out, lest one of his precious players should be left behind. If the passengers felt reassured by the hastily run repairs, they didn't show it. As they picked their way through the slush to the aircraft everyone seemed a little nervous and edgy. Many felt they were tempting providence to attempt a third take-off.

Verena Lukic was one; on hearing the call to board she began to have second thoughts. 'I was petrified,' she said. 'I decided to take a taxi to the train station, but Frank Taylor came up to me and said, "Mrs Lukic, the plane is ready. We must go to Manchester."' Clutching her baby, she followed him out across the apron to the waiting aircraft in the falling snow and darkening skies with an overwhelming feeling of dread.

But Taylor secretly had his own concerns about this third take-off attempt. As he climbed the steps he half turned and said to Albert Scanlon behind him, 'Sod this! In the RAF, if you didn't take off on the first attempt the flight was cancelled.' Albert, although nervous himself, said nothing, did what he was told and moved to the front of the cabin to sit down next to Bill Foulkes, ready to play cards.

Foulkes, who also had grave doubts, recalls the mood amongst the United party as they left the terminal for that fateful flight:

We were herded, like sheep, out to the plane for the final time. It seems ghoulish to recall, now, but some of us were joking about crashing, making remarks along the lines of 'Well, this is it boys.' There was definitely some anxiety in the air. All the time I was trying to remind myself how much I enjoyed flying. Yet again there was a delay, this time because a reporter, Alf Clarke from the *Evening Chronicle*, had hurried away to telephone a short story about the hold-up. He was subjected to some good-natured ribbing when he returned, rather breathlessly, and was strapped into his seat. By this time Kenny Morgans and David Pegg had left our little card school. I'm not sure where Kenny sat but David decided that he would be safer at the back of the plane. He went to join Mark Jones, Tommy Taylor and Eddie Colman.

Harry Gregg, trudging back to the aircraft with the sleet lashing his face, also had forebodings. He said:

I climbed the steps at the back of the aircraft and noticed that Tom Cable, the steward, had this time strapped himself into the seat at the rear. He looked scared. It wasn't a good sign when the crew looked worried.

I sat in a rearward facing seat on the right-hand side near the front, directly behind Bill Foulkes, and noticed his head protruding above the top of the seat and I thought, 'Hell, if anything goes wrong here, he's going to be decapitated.' I opened my shirt, tucked my collar down, and then opened my trousers to get comfortable. Then I put my feet up on the frame of the seat in front. Earlier in the trip I'd been reading a book called *The Whip*, by some bloke Roger McDonald. By today's standards *The Whip* was about as raunchy as *The Beano*, but having been brought up on a diet of hellfire and brimstone, it was playing on my conscience. I thought if anything happens here and I'm reading this it is straight to hell for me. I put the book away just before we started moving.

With the wipers slapping hypnotically across the cockpit windscreen, clearing the flakes of falling snow, Rayment called the tower.

Zulu Uniform: *609 Zulu Uniform, Munich tower. Would you have my clearance renewed, I am about ready to start.*
Tower: *Munchen tower, roger . . . B-line 609, cleared to start up engines. Your flight plan has been delivered to* ATC.

On the cramped flight deck Thain and Rayment once again went through the ritual of all the necessary pre-start-up checks on the instruments, radios and controls. Satisfied that all was in order, they started up the two Bristol Centaurus engines; in turn the 14-foot diameter propellers turned a few silent revolutions before coughing into life, sending a shudder through the airframe.

Zulu Uniform: *609 Zulu Uniform, I am ready to taxi, over.*
Tower: *609 Zulu Uniform, Munchen tower. Wind two nine zero, eight knots. Cleared to runway two five.* QNH *one zero zero four. Time five six and three quarters, over.*
Zulu Uniform: *Thank you.*

Standing on the apron, Bill Black raised his arm and gave the crew a thumbs up. The brakes were released and with a burst of throttle Zulu Uniform slowly taxied away from the terminal, the wheels leaving twin tracks in the freshly fallen snow. Again they had difficulty identifying the edge of the perimeter track owing to the ever-deepening layer of snow. Less than three minutes after leaving the terminal Zulu Uniform approached the runway holding point.

Zulu Uniform: *B-line 609 Zulu Uniform, are we cleared to line up?*
Tower: *B-line 609 Zulu Uniform, cleared to line up and hold, and here is your clearance, over.*
Zulu Uniform: *Roger, go ahead.*
Tower: *Munchen control clears B-line 609 to the Manchester airport via route as filed. Maintain one seven thousand feet. Right turn after take off, climb on south course inbound Freising range and maintain four thousand feet until further advised, over.*

The crew repeated the clearance back to the tower as they turned the Elizabethan onto the runway, and for the third time that afternoon lined up on the centre line of Runway 25. With the brakes set the engines were run up for a complete power check in preparation for take-off.

Tower: *B-line 609, what is your rate of climb? Over.*
Zulu Uniform: *Six hundred feet a minute.*

As Thain and Rayment went through the final cockpit checks another transmission from the tower interrupted their preparations.

Tower: *B-line 609, the clearance void if not airborne by zero four. Time now zero two.*

This gave Thain and Rayment exactly two minutes to decide whether to take off or return to the terminal. Did they feel under pressure? With two aborted take-offs already, they knew if they did not get the aircraft airborne in the next two minutes it was highly likely they would have to stop overnight at Munich. A brief discussion ensued between the two pilots and it was agreed that Thain would keep a careful eye on the engine instruments and control the throttle levers if any surging occurred while Rayment concentrated on handling the flying controls. At 3.03, their decision made, they called the tower.

Zulu Uniform: *Ah, Munich, Zulu Uniform is ready for take-off.*
Tower: *609, the wind three zero zero, one zero knots, cleared for take-off.*

Rayment, from the left-hand seat, slowly advanced the throttle levers with his right hand, followed through by Thain's left. At 28 inches of boost the brakes were released and the Elizabethan slowly began to roll down the runway. This time the acceleration was much slower than on the previous two take-off runs as the throttles were gradually inched forward to prevent surging. Once the throttles reached the stops, Thain tapped the back of Rayment's hand for him to relinquish control. Rayment then called out 'Check full power.' Thain, his eyes glued to the instruments, confirmed 'Full power set . . . temperatures and pressures OK. Warning lights out.' George Rodgers, the radio officer, from his station behind the pilots, pressed the transmit button and radioed the tower: 'Zulu Uniform rolling.'

As the Elizabethan sped down the runway the wheels threw up great whorls of brown slush, reminiscent of a flying-boat taking off. In the cockpit Thain called out to Rayment the increasing speeds . . . 60 knots . . . 70 knots . . . 80 knots . . . Then suddenly at 85 knots the port engine began surging again. Thain quickly reacted and pulled back the port throttle lever a little to arrest the surging and then gingerly pushed it forward again. The surging ceased and both engines sounded an even note.

Established on the take-off run, Rayment now transferred from nosewheel steering to rudder control as the rudders became fully effective in the gathering airflow. Not without some difficulty he pulled back the control column to raise the nosewheel free of the slush-covered runway in preparation for take-off. Meanwhile Thain had transferred his attention back to the airspeed indicator showing 105 knots with the needle edging sluggishly forward . . . 110 knots . . . 115 knots . . . At 117 knots Thain called out V1 (Velocity One, the point on the runway after which it isn't safe to abandon take-off). With Zulu Uniform committed to take-off Rayment listened intently for Thain's next call, V2, which would be at 119 knots — the minimum safe speed required to unstick and fly the aircraft safely off the ground.

At this point Zulu Uniform had covered two-thirds of the runway and was now entering the area of undisturbed slush unmarked by previous aircraft movements; the effect on the aircraft was dramatic. The needle wavered at 117 knots and then inexplicably dropped four or five knots. For the first time since the aircraft began its take-off run Thain, who was anticipating V2, was suddenly conscious of a distinct lack of acceleration and saw the needle drop further and flicker at 105. Rayment, now pulling hard back on the control column in a desperate effort to get airborne, yelled out above the roaring engines, 'CHRIST, WE WON'T MAKE IT!'

In the cabin the tension was palpable. Everyone had now stopped talking and sat in silence with their own thoughts. As the Elizabethan hurtled down the runway, many of the passengers felt all was not well with the aircraft. Bill Foulkes recalled:

I was hit by the strongest possible feeling of foreboding. Something told me we were not going to make it. It came to me that we should not be attempting to take off this third time in such terrible weather. By this time all the cards had stopped. I crouched right down, jamming my head into my chest, well below the level of my seat, and strapping myself in so tightly that I could hardly breathe. I have little doubt that these precautions saved my life.

As we accelerated down the runway I peered out of the window at the snow racing past. My last memory is of pushing the pack of cards hurriedly into my side pocket. The engines were surging but there was a peculiar note, as though they could not really get going, and the movement of the aircraft seemed decidedly sluggish. Then, just at the moment when we should have been getting off the ground, there was the first of a series of three sickening bumps. I just had time to think to myself, 'This is it' before I had the sensation of being thrown all over the place. Then there was darkness.

Just before the aircraft started to roll, Frank Taylor, sitting in his rearward facing seat, surreptitiously removed his small dental plate and slipped it in his pocket as a precaution in case anything went wrong. Looking down through the cabin window he watched the bow-wave of slush thrown up from the port wheel as the plane hurtled along. The lights on the runway edge flashed by, faster and faster until they were just a blur. With no sign of the aircraft lifting off, Taylor became anxious.

I felt certain we must be beyond the point of no return. I turned half right to look over my shoulder at the way ahead, as the machine tore on. I felt a sudden surge of alarm as, directly ahead, there was a wooden fence . . . *the perimeter fence.* I then saw the end of the runway and thought Christ, we're not going to make it. In that freezing moment I felt a sickening blow behind the left ear. At first I thought it was Frank Swift, for he often used to sneak up behind a pal to give a playful cuff behind the ear. Couldn't be Frank, he was yards away in the tail.

The thought didn't crystallise properly, for my senses were slipping away. It was like a tidal wave. Everything was becoming blurred and I was like a drowning man, fighting to keep his head above water. I had never been knocked out in my life before. So this is how it felt. Now there was a fierce buckling, and tremendous rending of metal with the machine shaking like a wild thing . . . then my eyes closed.

For Harry Gregg the first seeds of doubt about this flight occurred after the second aborted take-off. He felt no panic or any real fear; it was just an almost imperceptible sense that something bad was going to happen.

Directly across from me was a woman with a little girl and in front of them, on facing seats, the poker school. Roger Byrne, Johnny Berry and Liam Whelan sat on one side, and on the other, Ray Wood and Jackie Blanchflower. A vacant seat was intended for me.

All six of us had been playing poker the previous night and I virtually cleaned them out. I was intent on winding them up by refusing to give them a chance of getting their money back on the trip from Belgrade to Munich. They were giving me some stick over that, but the intention was to sit with them after we lifted out of Munich.

We rolled away once more and I glanced diagonally across to Roger Byrne. Roger wasn't a good flyer at the best of times and he looked petrified. I thought to myself, 'He's more scared than I am,' and I actually drew courage from his fear. The silence was punctuated by a nervous cough, then a snigger. Johnny Berry shouted, 'I don't know what you're laughing at. We're all going to get friggin' killed here!' Billy Whelan, a devout Roman Catholic, piped up, 'Well, if this is the time, then I'm ready.'

It takes a brave man to be a coward and if only someone had said at this point 'This is crazy!' or really raised an objection, then who knows?

Then we were off. This time I was glued to the window. The sensation as the wheels cut through the slush was of being in a speedboat. I watched as the telescopic rods of the undercarriage fully extended and the wheels began to lift off the ground. Bang! There was a sudden crash and debris began bombarding me on all sides. One second it was light, the next dark. There were no screams, no human sounds, only the terrible tearing of metal. Sparks burst all around. I felt something go up my nose. Then something cracked my skull like a hard-boiled egg. I was hit again at the front. The salty taste of blood was in my mouth and I was terrified to put my hands up to my head.

Zulu Uniform left the paved surface of the runway and rumbled on over the 250 yard grassed stopway, smashed through the perimeter fence, destroying part of the runway approach lighting, and then over a minor road, to the consternation of a German truck driver. Right up until Rayment called out his warning that they would not make it, Thain's eyes had not left the instruments. But now, for the first time since the take-off commenced, he looked up above the cockpit coaming, and there, framed in his cockpit window in the driving snow, was the appalling sight of a house and a tree directly in their path.

Thain raised his left hand and banged the throttle levers hard in an effort to gain more speed, but they were fully forward against the stops. Rayment, still desperately pulling hard back on the control column, yelled at Thain to retract the undercarriage in a desperate attempt to do something — anything — to get the aircraft off the ground. For a few seconds the aircraft's passage became smooth as if airborne and turned slowly to the right as Rayment deliberately made a vain attempt to avoid colliding with the house. Thain, gripping the coaming with both hands, saw that they couldn't possibly get between the house and the tree; with a stomach-churning realisation that a collision was inevitable he ducked his head below the instrument panel and braced himself as Zulu Uniform hurtled towards destruction.

Seconds later there was a murderous bang as the left wing scythed into the isolated house, ripping it away outboard of the engine, along with part of the tail unit. Fuel sprayed out from the ruptured wing tanks and the house immediately took fire. Inside Anna Winkler, the mother of four children, was sewing. Her husband was away, her eldest daughter was at a neighbour's house, and the two others were asleep. As fire engulfed the house she snatched the two sleeping children and threw them out into the snow; the other child, four-year-old Anna, made her escape from the burning building by crawling out through a window.

The shattered airliner, now spinning out of control, ploughed on past the house and struck the tree, smashing in the left-hand side of the cockpit where Rayment was seated. One hundred metres further on, the right-hand side of the fuselage aft of the trailing edge of the wings struck a small oil compound and wooden garage containing a truck loaded with drums of fuel. The impact completely severed the tail section and immediately the truck's fuel tank, along with the drums, exploded, enveloping the building and tail unit in flames, sending billowing black smoke skywards. The forward section of Zulu Uniform, its momentum carrying it onward, carved its way through the snow for a further 70 metres before coming to rest. Then, quite suddenly, the cacophony of tearing and breaking metal ceased. Fifty-four seconds after the throttles were opened, the sleek and graceful Elizabethan airliner now lay a broken and smouldering wreck in the falling snow, a mile from the main terminal. An eerie silence pervaded the scene of carnage. No one screamed for help, no one cried out. There was no noise at all . . . just absolute silence.

Chapter 9
Blood in the Snow

Thain, shaken and disorientated, sat strapped in his seat trying to gather his thoughts. On seeing the flicker of flames surrounding the aircraft he quickly came to his senses. Throwing off his harness, he gave the crew the order to evacuate the aircraft. The stewardesses Rosemary Cheverton and Margaret Bellis quickly made their escape by squeezing through the emergency window of the galley door which had blown out in the crash. Radio officer Rodgers quickly followed, pausing briefly to throw the battery master switch and circuit breakers, which could prove an additional fire hazard. Thain shouted to Rayment, 'Come on man, get out.' Rayment struggled to leave his seat but was helplessly trapped. He urged Thain to leave him and go on ahead. Thain squeezed through the same exit window and once on the ground saw a number of small fires attacking the aircraft. Fire had broken out in the stub of the port wing and another, more alarmingly, under the starboard engine, its wing tank still intact containing 500 gallons of volatile fuel. Fearing the risk of an imminent explosion, Thain yelled at the stewardesses and Rodgers to run for it. Thain, ignoring the danger, climbed back into the wreckage to grab the two handheld fire extinguishers, pausing long enough to tell Rayment that as soon as the fires had been tackled he would be back to help.

Inside the remains of the passenger cabin, Harry Gregg thought he had died. With a ringing head and bloody nose he lay motionless in the wreckage, trying to make sense of what had happened. He recalled:

An eerie stillness replaced the chaos, punctuated only by the interminable sound of hissing. All around was dark — it was as if I was frozen in time. Disorientated, a bulletin of random thoughts flashed through my mind. I've done well for the first time in my life . . . I won't see my little girl and wife . . . I won't see my mother and my family again . . . and I can't speak German. Then I noticed a shaft of light streaming down from just above me on the right.

Lying on his side, he unbuckled his seat belt and began to crawl towards the light. Sticking his head through the gaping hole in the fuselage he momentarily froze. There motionless on the ground in his air force blue suit lay Bert Whalley, the youth team coach. His eyes were open and there wasn't a mark on him. Gregg instinctively knew he was dead. Turning around in the cabin, despite the loss of one shoe, he kicked the hole bigger and dropped to the ground. He was confronted with a horrific scene: bodies lay everywhere in the snow and strewn all around was burning and blackened debris. It seemed impossible to Gregg that anyone had survived. 'I remember standing there on that chilling, snow-swept runway. I felt alone and helpless . . . and I was moaning to myself, "It's all gone, it's all finished."' With the smell of aviation fuel in the air and the crackle of fire, his first instinct was to run.

In the distance he saw the two stewardesses, George Rodgers, Peter Howard and Ted Ellyard running away from the scene; they half turned and urged him to run for it. Suddenly from around the nose of the aircraft Captain Thain appeared, clutching a fire extinguisher, and on seeing Gregg screamed at him, 'RUN YOU STUPID BASTARD, IT'S GOING TO EXPLODE!' Just then Gregg heard a cry and recalled the baby in the seat near him. He turned and roared at those fleeing, 'Come back you bastards, there are people alive in there.'

Gregg kicked at the wreckage and wormed his way back inside the fuselage. Scrabbling around in the darkness he came across a child's romper suit and was terrified of what he might find underneath it. But there was nothing there — no baby, no seat. On hearing a muffled cry he pushed deeper into the wreckage and there in the darkness, under a pile of debris, was the baby. Apart from a bad cut over one eye she seemed relatively unharmed. Crawling out of the wreckage cradling the child in his arms, he ran towards those who were running away. George Rodgers turned, came back and took the baby from him. Despite the imminent threat of the aircraft exploding Gregg clambered back into the aircraft again. Under a pile of wreckage he found Verena Lukic, the baby's mother, badly injured with a gaping wound to her eye. Sitting on his backside behind her, he pushed her along with his legs towards the opening and safety.

He then found goalkeeper Ray Wood trapped in the wreckage and tried to free him. Close by was Albert Scanlon, whose injuries were so severe that Gregg had to fight to prevent himself from being sick. Unable to free them, he came away thinking that both were dead and beyond help.

Dazed and disorientated, he began to wander about the immediate wreckage field searching for Jackie Blanchflower. They had been best friends since they played together as fourteen-year-old schoolboys for Ireland, and Gregg was desperate to find him. In his search he stumbled upon Bobby Charlton and Dennis Viollet, hanging half-in, half-out of the remains of the cabin. Dennis had a bad gash behind his right ear and both he and Bobby appeared to be dead. Nevertheless, he grabbed them by their trouser waistbands and dragged them 20 yards through the snow and slush away from the smouldering wreck.

Thain, now tackling the fire in the starboard engine on the other side of the aircraft, saw a dazed Bill Foulkes still sitting strapped in his seat near the jagged break in the fuselage, just staring blankly ahead. Banging on the cabin window he yelled at him, 'What the hell are you doing in there? Get out man, get out.' The seat in front of Foulkes, where teammate Albert Scanlon had been sitting, had disappeared where the cabin had been sliced in half at the cards table. Miraculously Foulkes had missed the break by inches. Reacting to Thain's urging, he attempted to get up but found he couldn't move. Realising he was still wearing his seat belt, he quickly unbuckled it and felt his legs, 'to see if they were still there'. Clambering out of the gaping hole he ran and ran in the ever-deepening snow. 'I remembered films I'd seen of engines exploding,' he said, 'and this passed through my mind as I ran. I must have covered 200 yards before I stopped.' When he turned round he couldn't believe the sight that met his eyes. He saw a trail of bodies in the snow that had been ejected from the aircraft as it split in two. The tail section was sticking out of the oil compound like a dart, burning fiercely and sending billowing black smoke skyward, and everywhere there were explosions. He looked down at his feet and saw he had no shoes on and wondered why. Suddenly he became aware of a crowd of confused jabbering people, mostly German women crowding round him who at first couldn't believe he was a survivor. Recovering from his initial panic, a dazed Foulkes eventually made his way back to the scene of devastation and teamed up with Peter Howard, Ted Ellyard and the stewardesses in the search for survivors.

Meanwhile Harry Gregg, continuing his search for Jackie, came across Matt Busby halfway between the main wreckage and the burning building. Semi-conscious and profoundly shocked, Busby sat slumped in the snow moaning, painfully holding his chest, with his legs stretched out in front of him. All around him in the snow and slush lay the remains of his Babes — dead, dying or grievously injured. Gregg propped him up with some wreckage and tried to reassure him before leaving to continue his search for Jackie. About thirty yards further on he found him lying in a pool of melted snow, crying out that he had broken his back and was paralysed. His inability to move was due to the fact that his captain, Roger Byrne, was draped across his waist. Roger was dead. There wasn't a mark on him and his eyes were open. Harry Gregg to this day has always regretted that he didn't close his eyes. Harry did his best to comfort and reassure Jackie that he was okay. Shocked to see that the lower part of his right arm was almost severed at the elbow, he took off his tie to make a tourniquet to staunch the flow of blood. Pulling it too tight, it snapped and in desperation he scrabbled around in the mud and slush for something else. He then became aware that someone was standing behind him; he half turned and looked up to see one of the stewardesses staring blankly at him. He screamed at her, 'Get me something to tie his arm.' She didn't react; she just stood there rooted to the spot and stared back at him in shock.

Jackie Blanchflower never lost consciousness and remembers everything that happened when the aircraft left the runway and broke up. He said, 'It was like going down a cobbled road. The plane broke in half at the card tables and I was thrown out of the top. I saw the front of the aircraft twisting round, then it stopped and fires began to break out. Roger was lying across my legs with his eyes open. I just lay there watching the second hand of his watch tick by. I started to talk to him . . . then Harry came.'

Gregg, kneeling beside his teammate, remembers a terrified German doctor, clad in a tweed coat and wellington boots, arriving on the scene. Producing a hypodermic syringe from his bag, he ran from body to body in a panic. Gregg, who spoke no German, tried his best to communicate with him to come and help Jackie, but every time there was an explosion he turned tail and ran. Then, after one enormous blast, he watched bemused as the doctor was hurled in the air, 'landing on his arse and still holding the syringe in the air like the Statue of Liberty'.

As Harry tended to Jackie he got the biggest shock so far when he turned to see Bobby Charlton and Dennis Viollet standing close by, as if they had just awakened from sleep, staring in a daze at the burning wreckage. He couldn't believe they were alive. After what seemed an eternity a battered Volkswagen minibus, in which the rear seats had been removed for use as a coal wagon, came bouncing across the field towards them. The able-bodied survivors helped to get Busby into the rear of the vehicle along with Jackie Blanchflower and the badly injured Johnny Berry. The driver motioned to Bill Foulkes and Dennis Viollet to sit up front with him while Harry Gregg and Bobby Charlton climbed in behind. They set off bumping and lurching over the snow. After a few yards someone ran out in front of the truck to stop them to pick up

Maria Miklos, wife of the travel courier, who was severely burned. The driver, who after this short delay was anxious to get to the hospital at all speed, put his foot down and shot off, swerving and skidding all over the place. Bill Foulkes berated the driver to slow down but to no avail, and fearful of a crash resorted to punching him on the back of his head. But the driver took no notice and continued his headlong mercy dash through the streets of Munich.

Back at the crash scene Peter Howard and Ted Ellyard, sifting through the twisted remains of the cabin for survivors, came across the familiar face of fellow journalist Frank Taylor. He was in a dreadful state. His left elbow was pulped and his right leg just above the ankle was smashed, with the broken ends of the tibia and fibula protruding though the trouser leg. As they gently eased him out of the rent in the fuselage and laid him on the ground, the semi-conscious Taylor mumbled to himself, 'What a bloody silly way to die.'

Howard was still not finished, and along with Rodgers, the radio officer, made another sortie back into the wreckage. Then, just as his hopes of finding any more survivors faded and he was about to leave, he saw a movement under a pile of debris. It was Kenny Morgans, the youngest of the Babes, unconscious but still alive. Howard, shocked and exhausted, handed over to the rescuers who were now arriving on the scene in increasing numbers. Eventually he made his way back to the airport terminal to seek out a telephone and call his paper. Having lived through the horrors of the crash he gave them, like the good journalist he was, the facts. He told them of the bravery of Harry Gregg; of his colleague, Ted Ellyard; the stewardesses Bellis and Cheverton; of what Captain Thain and his radio officer did. But being the modest chap he was, Peter Howard said very little in his dispatches about Peter Howard.

It took an extraordinary amount of time before the rescue services arrived on the scene. The airport fire brigade initially went to the wrong side of the airfield, and then were held up because of a locked gate. When they finally arrived they quickly brought the remaining fires under control. But the enormity of the disaster caught the firemen on the hop without sufficient blankets to cover the bodies. An airport official ordered them to strip all the seat covers off the cars in the VIP car park to use as makeshift shrouds. 'It was dreadful,' said one, 'especially when we returned from the mortuary and the same official ordered us to go back and retrieve the covers and replace them back in the cars.'

While all this was going on Rayment remained trapped in his seat on the flight deck. Attempts to free him from the inside of the wrecked fuselage failed, and in frustration Thain borrowed an axe from a fireman and made a futile attempt to hack his way through the side of the nose section. In the end rescuers were forced to climb along the starboard wing to the top of the cockpit and cut him free from the tangle of metal.

A few miles away at Munich's Rechts der Isar Hospital, the chief surgeon, Professor Georg Maurer, was doing his afternoon rounds on the wards. From the early morning he had undertaken and supervised some twenty-five operations, yet he showed not the slightest sign of fatigue. The professor was a short, portly man with a friendly face from which warm brown eyes peered out mischievously through rimless spectacles. He was admired, respected and loved by all the hospital staff. It was hard to believe, looking at this mild-mannered man, that eighteen years earlier he had been decorated with the Iron Cross for his work and bravery tending the wounded of both German and allied soldiers on the bloody beaches of Dunkirk. As he walked down the hospital corridor, with his white-coated entourage following closely behind, a hospital orderly rushed up and exclaimed: '*Herr Professor . . . Flugzeut catastrophe at Riem!*'

From the moment he was given the news, Maurer and his staff had everything under control. The emergency plan that the hospital had practised for many years, now stark reality, swung into action with typical German efficiency. Doctors, surgeons and consultants were called in and scrubbed up in readiness. Trolleys for setting up infusions and transfusions were made ready, the blood bank was alerted and all off duty was cancelled, while porters in the casualty department waited expectantly to receive the injured and transport them upstairs to the theatres.

Even the medical students from the hospital college were called in to help. Professor Maurer's son Peter, who was one, recalled:

> There was a feeling of total grief and horror, but also sheer disbelief that this world famous team of young stars had crashed in our own back gardens. It was like a state of emergency — there was a call for all hands on deck and we rushed down from the college through the snow to help out. We didn't get any sleep for forty-eight hours, and it felt like the whole country was involved. We had to have some specialist equipment shipped in all the way from Freiburg in south-west Germany to treat the serious injuries. Even before the plane crash my father was a much respected and well connected figure, but you could say that the tragic events of February 1958 created some friendships for life.

The battered Volkswagen carrying Harry Gregg, Bill Foulkes, Dennis Viollet, Bobby Charlton and the critically injured sped through the gates of the garden-surrounded Rechts der Isar Hospital and screeched to a halt in front of the main entrance. Soon after, a convoy of ambulances carrying the rest of the casualties began to arrive. It was a chaotic scene as stretcher after stretcher with the injured and dying was carried into the hospital where doctors, surgeons and nurses battled to cope with the enormity of the disaster. But it was too late for some. Frank Swift, severely burned in the accident, died as he was carried through the doors — he was forty-three and a few days old. Matt Busby, who was critically injured, hovered close to death; he was administered the last rites twice by a Roman Catholic priest.

Gregg and Foulkes were called upon by the hospital staff to identify people as they were being treated. Harry Gregg remembers being shocked when he was called in to see Ray Wood, who was in a dreadful state with his eye hanging out of its socket; Gregg thought he was dead. It was the same for Bill Foulkes — when he was asked to identify a man on a bed whose face was in a terrible mess, he recognised him as his teammate Johnny Berry.

Eventually a group of nurses, brandishing syringes, herded Harry Gregg, Bill Foulkes, Bobby Charlton, Peter Howard and Ted Ellyard down a corridor for treatment. Nebosja Tomasevich, the Yugoslav diplomat on the aircraft, who in a daze had tagged on to the group, suddenly collapsed and slid down the wall. It turned out that he had broken his leg in the crash and it was a wonder to everyone how he managed to stay upright for so long. Bobby Charlton was given a jab and was soon flat out on a trolley. But Harry Gregg and Bill Foulkes were having none of it; protesting they were perfectly okay they decided to leave the hospital. A female representative from BEA had now arrived and escorted them to the Stathus Hotel in the town, along with Peter Howard and Ted Ellyard. It was there that Harry Gregg remembers standing by the window of his hotel room, 'for what seemed like an eternity. Bewildered by what had just happened I stared as the cars in the street below gradually disappeared under a blanket of snow.' In that same room Bill Foulkes tasted his first whisky and puffed on his first cigarette.

Back at the crash scene Captain Thain, under protest, was eventually led away and driven to the airport terminal. Before he left he looked up at the battered cockpit and gave Rayment a 'thumbs up'. His friend smiled weakly back, calmly waiting to be rescued. 'I came away,' said Thain, 'quite certain he would be all right.'

Sitting in the BEA office in the terminal building he was given a cup of coffee and a plaster was put on his bleeding knuckles — a stark reminder, not of the crash, but of the first abandoned take-off. He asked another BEA pilot, who had just landed on his way back to the UK, to telephone the relatives of the crew and give them the news first-hand when he arrived back in London. Thain then put in a call to the authorities in London to officially report the accident.

Left alone in the room, he sipped on his coffee and pondered on the events leading up to the accident. The predominant thought going round and round in his head was why had they crashed? Before Rayment had cried out that they wouldn't make it, both engines were running at full throttle, with no indication of boost surging. So what had caused them to lose speed, when all the laws of aerodynamics dictated that they should have continued to accelerate and take off? He hoped to have the opportunity to discuss the problem later with Rayment.

Apart from being somewhat shaken and shocked, Thain was uninjured; nevertheless he was taken by car to the hospital to be checked over. On arrival he was stunned to learn from a doctor that Rayment had been brought in with critical injuries and it was touch and go whether he would pull through. Unable to discuss the events leading up to the crash with his fellow captain, he left for the hotel where the other survivors had been taken. There in the quiet of his room the full enormity of the disaster suddenly hit him and with a wave of emotion he burst into tears.

Later, having composed himself, he was joined in the room by the rest of his crew, along with Harry Gregg, Bill Foulkes and the others for a meal; understandably, no one felt much like eating. With the dreadful events of the day still fresh in his mind, Thain talked through with his attentive audience the procedure of that last catastrophic take-off, and proffered his theory that slush on the runway may have caused the accident. Later, when everyone retired, the crew gathered in Thain's room where they were joined by the Chief Pilot of BEA, Captain Baillie, who had just flown in from London, and once again Thain went through all the harrowing details.

It was the first fatal crash of an Elizabethan airliner, which had carried 2,340,000 passengers on 86,000 flights since it began operations with BEA in 1952. As international aviation law dictated, the country where the accident occurred 'will institute an inquiry into the circumstances of the accident'. This task fell to the Luftfahrt Bundesamt accident investigation team based in Brunswick. Headed by Chief Inspector of Accidents Captain Hans J. Reichel, the investigating team immediately flew out to Munich to begin their inquiries. Reichel was fifty-seven, an experienced pilot with 1,500,000 miles flown in a career that began in 1924 with the German national airline Lufthansa. During the Spanish Civil War he saw service as a supply pilot for the German Condor Legion and flew as a transport officer in the Second World War. During the long flight to Munich, Reichel looked out into the night watching the snow streak past his window. It was then that the notion occurred to him that ice on the wings could have caused the accident. Whether this was true or not, the idea was certainly planted firmly in his mind.

Reichel's aircraft landed at Munich shortly before 10 p.m. local time, some six hours after the crash, and he was immediately driven out to the crash site by airport officials, who on the short journey discussed with him their own theory that ice on the wings could have been a factor that caused the accident. Arriving at the scene in pitch darkness Reichel now had the expectation of finding ice on the wings — and he found it!

In the hours since the crash the weather had further deteriorated and heavy snow fell continuously. Little or no provision had been made to preserve the evidence at the scene and reporters, photographers, airport officials, firemen and spectators trampled all over the site. No lighting had been secured to illuminate the wreckage for the investigators and battery lamps had to be commandeered from a BBC news cameraman. Reichel approached the remains of Zulu Uniform and without hesitation went straight to the intact starboard wing and described what he found.

The wrecked aircraft was covered with a layer of snow about eight centimetres thick. The right wing, which was only slightly damaged, was still firmly attached to the fuselage and had not been exposed to the effects of fire, presented a completely even layer of snow. This was powdery and could be brushed aside with the hand without difficulty. Under this there was a layer of ice, the upper surfaces of which were very rough, frozen firmly onto the skin of the wing. When one ran one's hand over it, it felt like a coarse kitchen grater. The very loose powdery snow lying on top had not blended at all with the layer of ice. It could, for example, be blown off without difficulty, so as to leave the bare layer of ice exposed. I found the same condition at all points on the wing, which was examined thoroughly, with the exception of the part situated above the engine nacelle and in the region of the slipstream. Here, after the snow had been removed, the bare outer skin was visible, without any ice accretion. Apart from this icing I could find nothing which might have been a cause of the accident, or could be considered to have contributed to it.

Reichel further noted that the propeller blades were set in the take-off pitch angle, the throttle levers were in the fully open position and the main undercarriage was down. With this cursory examination he came away from the scene with his mind made up — the cause of the crash was wing icing. He made no attempt to examine the scene in daylight and if it wasn't for the protestations of other interested parties he would have had the wreckage disposed of the following day.

In London, when news of the disaster broke, a BEA accident investigation team was hastily convened and departed immediately for Munich. The party included the chief executive of BEA, Antony Milward; the chief pilot, Captain Baillie; the chief accident investigator, J. W. Gibbs; the director of flight operations, Captain James; and two BEA doctors. Despite the appalling weather they managed to land at Munich at the same time Reichel was making his nocturnal examination of the remains of Zulu Uniform.

Also alerted was G. M. (Ned) Kelly of the Accident Investigation Branch (AIB) Farnborough, who would act as the accredited British representative in the forthcoming inquiry. After service in the RAF Kelly, like Thain, had joined BEA as a pilot and eventually became a senior captain on Elizabethans; he had flown with Thain as first officer on several occasions. However, his flying career was prematurely cut short by the deterioration of his hearing and he became safety officer on the Elizabethan flight before transferring to the AIB in 1955. Unable to travel with the main BEA party, he set out for Munich the following morning, but owing to the deteriorating weather his aircraft was diverted to Frankfurt and he completed his journey by train, arriving at 11 p.m.

The Germans, convinced they had solved the mystery of the crash, were quick to issue a statement which was printed in *The Times*: 'After preliminary investigation, the fact that the aircraft did not leave the ground was probably the result of ice on the wings.' They also added that Captain Thain had not given a satisfactory explanation of why he did not discontinue the final attempt to take off. It seemed from the start of the investigation the Germans were prepared to show an early hand, insisting that ice on the wings had caused the accident — a view that, as time progressed, they would find difficult to retreat from.

It did not help matters when a few days later the director of Munich Airport, Count Rudolph zu Castell, told a press conference that 'icing on the wings had been established beyond all doubt'. His remarks were not surprising, in that the condition of the aircraft is the captain's responsibility and the condition of the runway is the airport authority's. It seemed at this early stage in the investigation that Castell was trying desperately to keep his head clear of the chopping block. Thain's union, BALPA, reacted angrily to these statements and demanded that all lines of inquiry should be followed up before any more irresponsible comments were made imputing the blame on Thain, when there was not the slightest foundation for the remarks at this early stage of the investigation.

J. W. Gibbs, the BEA chief accident investigator, from his own inquiries, was now moving towards the view expressed by Captain Thain, Bill Black and G. M. Kelly — that the condition of the runway was a decisive factor in the cause of the accident — and none of them were surprised when within days of the crash other incidents from BEA pilots began to surface.

One of the most dramatic and alarming came from the captain of an empty BEA Viscount on a positioning flight from Manchester to London. At the time the runway at Ringway was covered in a thick layer of soft slush and the pilot was concerned enough to drive out in the controller's van to inspect it. He noted that the temperature was above freezing and parts of the tarmac were showing through the thawing slush. In the absence of any guidelines from the airline regarding such conditions, he made the decision to take off.

As I charged down the runway I noticed fluctuations in the acceleration, but was unable to exceed 90 knots (V1 would have been about 98 knots and V2, 108 knots). About two-thirds of the way down the runway the speed decelerated to 85 knots, and I hauled the nosewheel off the ground. The speed immediately built up and we unstuck. What was particularly noticeable was the marked surge of acceleration, indicating the large amount of drag which had been on the main wheels, even with the nosewheel clear of the deck. I gathered together — in fact we all did — our shattered nerves, and flew back to London. I certainly appreciated this behaviour of the tricycle under-carriage in slush, but due to my lack of experience on the type, did not realise the dangerous drag effect on the nosewheel in particular.

The first reported incident involving a BEA Elizabethan on a slush-covered runway was reported as far back as January 1955, and although the pilots involved submitted a detailed report to BEA, the airline filed it away and did nothing. In the Elizabethan flying manual there was no warning or guidance for pilots regarding landing and taking off from snow- and slush-covered runways. It was suggested by flight crews that BEA should undertake some research of its own into the matter to give captains some factual information on the retarding effects of slush on aircraft performance. Again BEA did nothing. After the Munich crash and the disturbing news of other incidents, BEA pilots were rightly angered to discover that the Dutch airline KLM had for the past four years been giving their pilots strict guidelines about taking off in slush. One KLM document issued to its flight crews gave the following advice:

Take-offs in snow and slush: Do not attempt to take-off in tricycle aircraft, when slush or wet snow is more than two inches deep on the runway.

The increased resistance due to slush, which varies according to the speed of the aircraft, may reach such a value that it equals the available thrust and prevents further acceleration.

Pitching movement on the nosewheel may also build up so rapidly that it cannot be controlled by the elevators. If the nosewheel is difficult to lift, it is a sign of danger, and the take-off should be discontinued immediately.

Thain, along with his crew, flew home on the evening of Saturday 8 February, two days after the accident. He was now news and a horde of reporters was waiting for him at Heathrow. Thain was quite prepared to be interviewed by the press but BEA, as if ashamed of him, tried to smuggle him out of the aircraft by the crew door. But the press caught on and as Thain and his crew walked down the steps they were met with a barrage of flashbulbs. He later gave a short statement to a reporter from *The Times* newspaper:

I cannot give the cause of the disaster, but what would have been a simple mishap, in which passengers might have climbed out of the aircraft with ankle injuries, was turned into a major disaster by the house situated three hundred yards from the end of the Munich Airport runway. Let us say that the house should not have been there.

Now back home, BEA informed him that under the circumstances he was deemed unfit for flying duties and told to take some time off. When the period of leave expired the airline promptly suspended him on full pay until further notice. Thain was not unduly worried by this turn of events. He truly believed that the accident was not due to any failure of duty on his or Rayment's part and the cause lay in some external factor beyond their control. He had faith that the forthcoming inquiry would, on all the available evidence, clear him of any blame. In the meantime,

Thain sent Reichel a copy of his own formal report and as much documentation he could lay his hands on dealing with research into slush and its effects on aircraft performance. With that he waited in confidence for the inquiry to open in April.

Chapter 10
Dealing with Disaster

As the terrible events unfolded at the end of the runway in Munich, Jimmy Murphy was on a train travelling back to Manchester from Cardiff. He was a happy and contented man. The previous day he had watched his Welsh team defeat Israel at Ninian Park to win through to their first World Cup final — an outstanding achievement brought about by Murphy's enthusiasm and passion for his national side. It had been a tough match with the Welshmen leaving it until the last ten minutes of the game to score, with Ivor Allchurch and Cliff Jones netting a goal apiece.

Murphy had told Busby before the team flew off to Belgrade that he would prefer to travel with the United party rather than attend the international in Cardiff. But Matt told him that his duty lay with the Welsh team. 'I always sat next to Matt on our European trips,' Murphy recalled, 'but I did what he said and let him go off to Red Star without me. Mind you, I've got to be honest; my mind was more on our game in Yugoslavia than the match I was watching. When I heard the news that we were through to the semi-finals it was great load off my mind. I didn't like not being there.'

Oblivious of what had happened in Munich just a few hours earlier, he stepped off the train at Manchester's London Road station in the late afternoon; it was freezing cold with snow falling from a leaden sky. Instead of going home he jumped into a taxi and headed straight for Old Trafford. It had been a hectic few days for him and the club and there was much for him to do before he could go home. His attention now switched from the Welsh team to his beloved United and the top-of-the-table clash with Wolves on the coming Saturday. He wanted to be there to greet Busby and the players on their return and see if anyone was injured. Arriving at the ground, he set off whistling down the corridor to his office only to be stopped by Alma George, Matt Busby's secretary. Aware that he knew nothing of the tragedy she broke the news as best as she could that the charter flight had crashed. Murphy failed to react. He just stood there rooted to the spot, not comprehending the enormity of what was being said to him. 'She told me again. It still didn't sink in, and then she started to cry. She said many people had died . . . some of the players. I couldn't believe it. The words seemed to ring in my head. Alma left me and I went to my office. My head was in a state of confusion and I started to cry. The numbing horror of that moment will never leave me until my death.'

Sitting at his desk trying to compose himself, Murphy picked up the telephone and called the police, the press, the BBC and anyone he could think of that could give him some information as to what had happened. In the coming hours the full extent of the devastating disaster slowly unfolded. By midnight he knew that his precious players Roger Byrne, Tommy Taylor, David Pegg, Billy Whelan, Geoff Bent, Eddie Colman and Mark Jones were dead. He was shocked even further with the news that the club secretary, Walter Crickmer, and his two closest friends, Bert Whalley and Tom Curry, had also perished, and Matt Busby and Duncan Edwards were fighting for their lives. Murphy felt empty and lost; he knew Old Trafford would never be the same again. It was the early hours when Murphy finally left a dark and deserted Old Trafford for home. Sleep was out of the question and he ended up sitting alone with his thoughts at the kitchen table, chain-smoking and downing a bottle of whisky.

After the two abandoned take-offs, Alf Clarke of the *Manchester Evening Chronicle* scurried off to find a phone in the terminal building and rang his sports desk to say that the weather was worsening and the flight was held up, with the possibility of being stranded for the night. By three o'clock his paper and its sister, the *Manchester Evening News*, had more or less been put to bed with the final editions coming off the presses at Withy Grove. Then, at around 3.30 p.m. a Press Association 'flash' on the teleprinter gave the unbelievable news: 'MANCHESTER UNITED AIRCRAFT CRASHED ON TAKE-OFF . . . HEAVY LOSS OF LIFE FEARED.' The BBC broke into its afternoon radio programmes with a news bulletin that told a similar story. People, not only in Manchester but all over the country, stopped what they were doing, took a deep breath and tried to comprehend the words they were being told. Everyone loved the Babes, they were young and confident, full of fun, great players, a great team — it was a national disaster.

In the newspaper offices reporters who were due to go off duty stayed behind as editors hastily arranged conferences. Soon the presses were spewing out extra editions that sold out as fast as they could be printed. Tom Jackson's match report wired from Belgrade had already been printed on the back page — part of it read with mocking irony, 'United will never have a tougher fight than this'.

In Manchester the news quickly spread mouth to mouth as the factories and offices turned out with men streaming onto the streets heading for the news vendors for every scrap of information. Children ran home from school to ask their mothers if the rumours they had heard were true, that their footballing heroes were no more. As the hours passed the list of casualties steadily grew and it finally hit home to the fans that their team had died, along with the realisation that the exuberant, brilliant Babes would never grace the Old Trafford turf again. For the people of Manchester the grief was personal. People numb with shock and disbelief wept openly on the streets, in shops, on buses, at home; all of them would remember for the rest of their lives where they were and what they were doing when they first heard the devastating news. The majority of people had never seen the Babes play, but this tragedy touched them all.

Wilf McGuinness, a Babe himself, who had not yet established himself in the first team, clearly remembers how he heard the news. He was walking down Princess Street in Manchester city centre when he spotted a news billboard shouting the words: 'PLANE CRASH'.

There wasn't much news at that time — at first we were told the plane had crashed on the runway. But I knew someone at the Daily Dispatch offices so I decided to go there and find out more. It was only then that I discovered there were fatalities. I stayed at the offices for some time as the list of survivors was announced.

It was just horrendous — I remember praying that everybody would be all right. They were great friends. You can imagine how the whole of Manchester felt, and they didn't even know the victims. I was in a state of shock, and for weeks afterwards I couldn't come to terms with it. I don't think anybody could.

The wives, girlfriends and relatives of the players heard the devastating news in various ways. Joy Byrne had been waiting at home for Roger to return to tell him the news that she had fallen pregnant with their first child. Then at teatime a newsflash came on the radio giving brief details. Roger's parents immediately came round to be with her, and along with numerous relatives and friends spent the rest of the evening waiting. They sat watching the TV and listened to the radio as each news bulletin gave further details of who had died and who had survived. Then at midnight she received the telephone call she had been dreading — Roger was dead. They had been married just six months. Thirty-eight weeks later she gave birth to a son. She christened him Roger.

June, the wife of half-back Mark Jones, was in a shop buying cream cakes for his return when she heard the news about the accident. 'I just stood there,' she said, 'and when the woman in the shop saw the look on my face, she must have known something was wrong. She asked me whatever was the matter and I told her my husband was on the plane.' It was six agonising hours later before she learned the worst from the United coach, Joe Armstrong. In a state of nervous panic she rushed upstairs, grabbed her son out of his cot and ran out of the house into the street, clutching her child, before someone brought her back.

It was fate that took Geoff Bent to his death. He only went along as cover for the injured Roger Byrne. As it turned out Roger was declared fit and Geoff never played and travelled to Belgrade as a passenger. Geoff had a sense of foreboding about the trip and he made it known to Busby that he didn't want to be included in the team selection. But his wife Marion, who had recently given birth to their first child, persuaded him to go off with his pals and enjoy himself. Forever after she blamed herself for his death.

For the staff in the Manchester newspaper offices it was the same, as the appalling news slowly filtered through that eight of their close friends and colleagues had lost their lives in the disaster. Hard-bitten journalists, used to reporting tragedy, now found themselves making it. All they could do now was to sit down with a heavy heart and write their obituaries.

The following morning the bold headlines of the disaster were emblazoned on every front page of every newspaper in the country. Overnight the enormity of the tragedy became clear with the papers reporting twenty-one dead, including seven players, eight journalists and six passengers. The Lord Mayor of Manchester, Leslie Lever, cancelled all his engagements and opened a disaster fund. Contributions poured in from the public and businesses across the city; even the inmates of Strangeways Prison chipped in. In the following days contributions came in from every corner of the country; by 15 February, nine days after the accident, the disaster fund had surpassed £8,000.

Besides condolences from the Queen, messages of sympathy arrived from all over the world, including President Tito of Yugoslavia and the German Chancellor. The president of Red Star suggested that United should be given the title of honorary champions of the European Cup for 1958, and the Yugoslav newspaper *Sport* went so far as to propose that the European Cup should be renamed the Manchester United Cup.

The morning after the accident BEA organised a mercy flight from Ringway Airport to fly the relatives and friends out to Munich via Paris. On board the aircraft was a distraught Jimmy

Murphy, who like everybody else was paralysed with grief and close to tears. When Jimmy walked into the hospital he entered a nightmare world. He was stunned by what he saw. 'It was a terrible, terrible time,' he said looking around at his stricken players.

Matt Busby lay ashen in an oxygen tent; he told Jimmy to 'keep the flag flying'. Elsewhere in the ward were the surviving members of the team: Dennis Viollet, Ray Wood, Albert Scanlon, Kenny Morgans, Bobby Charlton and Jackie Blanchflower. The most seriously injured was Johnny Berry, who lay in a coma in a separate room on the floor above. Jimmy, although grief-stricken, put on a brave face as he went from bed to bed, joking and chatting with his boys to keep their spirits up. He then went over and stood at Duncan's bedside. Ill as he was, the Babes' star player momentarily opened his eyes in recognition and whispered, 'Hello Jimmy. What time's kick-off on Saturday?' 'Usual time Dunc . . . three o'clock.' 'I'll get stuck in Jimmy,' he told him. Murphy, with tears rolling down his cheeks, replied, 'I know you will son . . . I know.' With that Duncan closed his eyes and lapsed into unconsciousness.

Also lying in the hospital was Kenneth Rayment. After being cut from the wreckage he had arrived at the hospital critically injured and was given an immediate tracheotomy and put in an oxygen tent to help his breathing. On the evening of the crash he lapsed into a coma from which he never recovered. On 18 March his body was flown back to London.

Bill Foulkes recalls returning to the hospital with Harry Gregg the following day. It was then that the full horror of the disaster became shockingly clear. 'We didn't say much to any of them, the situation was beyond anything but the briefest of words. I was just beginning to think it didn't look too bad. When I asked a nurse where we should go to see the rest of the lads, she looked puzzled, so I asked her again, and she said there were no others. She said the only survivors were the ones I had seen in that hospital. That was when it hit me. All I wanted to do was to go home. It took me a long, long time to recover from that moment.'

Later that night in the lobby of the Stathus Hotel, Harry Gregg and Bill Foulkes waited for the lift to take them to their room. Harry turned to Bill and told him he couldn't be bothered to wait and would walk up instead. As he approached the top of the stairs he heard a deep sobbing noise, and as he turned he came upon Jimmy Murphy sitting alone on the stairs in the darkness, crying his heart out. Gregg momentarily hesitated, decided not to disturb him and turned away unnoticed.

The following day Harry Gregg and Bill Foulkes returned to the crash site and rummaged about the remains of the cabin. Bill wandered over to that part of the wreckage where he had been sitting and was amazed to find a bottle of gin given to him at the post-match party unbroken; above in the luggage rack, neatly folded, was his overcoat. An official led them away from the depressing scene and took them to the terminal for a stiff drink and to retrieve what was left of their salvaged luggage.

After a final visit to the hospital, Jimmy Murphy decided to get Gregg and Foulkes away from the hell of Munich and back home. Although BEA had insensitively offered to fly them back at their own expense, it was decided to travel back overland by train and ferry. The journey was a nightmare for both players — every time the train braked it brought flashbacks of that final take-off attempt down the slush-covered runway. When their boat docked in Harwich they were met by a posse of reporters, but with very little luggage they quickly slipped through customs and boarded the train to London, where on arrival they saw the largest gathering of reporters and photographers they had ever seen. Led away by the police they were soon reunited with their wives in a London hotel.

Just before dawn on the following Monday, twenty-one coffins of pale elm, each draped with the Union Jack, passed through Munich's silent streets on the journey to the airport where, without ceremony, they were loaded on board a specially chartered BEA Viscount freighter. Later in the afternoon, following a service for the victims attended by the British Consul, Munich City Police officers formed a guard of honour as representatives of the Bavarian State Government and the City of Munich watched in silence as countless floral tributes were handed over to the crew to place inside the aircraft. Sepp Herberger from the West German

Football Association presented a wreath on behalf of all the German soccer clubs. The final tribute came from the ground staff of Munich-Riem Airport, who handed their own bouquet to the airliner steward.

At three o'clock the engines burst into life and the airliner slowly taxied away from the terminal building. Lining up on the same runway that Zulu Uniform had commenced its final disastrous take-off from four days earlier, the Viscount's engines screamed at full throttle, slipped its brakes, sped down the runway and gracefully lifted off into the late afternoon sunshine, passing low over the wreckage of Zulu Uniform.

The Babes were going home.

After a brief stop-over at London where four coffins were removed, the aircraft took-off on the final leg to Manchester. At Ringway Airport huge crowds had patiently gathered throughout the day, waiting to witness the sad return of their heroes. Despite the rain and the flight running two hours late, it did nothing to lessen the numbers keeping vigil. Then, at just after ten o'clock, the landing lights of the Viscount stabbed the black night sky as it turned onto the approach and slowly began its descent towards the runway.

The aircraft taxied to a halt in front of the terminal building where the Lord Mayor of Manchester, Alderman Leslie Lever, and United directors Harold Hardman, William Petherbridge and the recently appointed Louis Edwards stood in silence with their heads bowed. The cabin door opened and fifty-eight wreaths of red carnations and white tulips were carried down the steps, followed by the coffin of captain Roger Byrne and those of his teammates and United officials.

Eventually a convoy of hearses, saluted by airport personnel, turned out of the airport gates onto Ringway Road on the start of its long, slow journey to Old Trafford. One estimate put the crowds lining the route at 100,000. Besides those wearing red and white scarves and rosettes, who had stood on the terraces and watched the Babes every Saturday, there were thousands more who had never seen them play but just wanted to be there. All along the route to the ground, despite the falling rain, the roads were crowded with mourners: housewives in headscarves, mothers holding young children, Teddy boys, men in cloth caps, office girls, schoolboy fans clutching pictures of their fallen heroes. They all waited at the kerbside, with sadness showing on every face as they paid a tearful homage to the Babes' last ride home. The city that had cheered their young stars on now cried as they came back in coffins.

It was past midnight when the cortège finally arrived at the main entrance to the ground, where the crowd was most concentrated. Mounted police did their best to control the vast throngs that at one point threatened to breach the cordon. One by one the coffins were offloaded from the hearses and carried through the large wooden doors to lie in the gymnasium under the main grandstand, just yards from the pitch where they once entertained the fans with their footballing skills.

Manchester Police Constable Tom Potter, who along with a colleague was detailed to guard the coffins, has never got over his all-night vigil. He recalled:

When they brought them home the streets were crowded but there was hardly a sound. All you heard was the wheels on the road and grown men crying. The coffins were taken into a small gymnasium used as a chapel of rest, and the two of us were locked inside the stadium for what was going to be a long, long night. The other constable looked at me and there were tears in his eyes. Throughout the night people were coming to the door outside leaving flowers and crying and praying. All night long, I smelled the fresh varnish of those coffins and it's still with me today. Whenever I smell new varnish I think of those coffins in that gymnasium and seeing them with tears in my eyes. I couldn't wait to go home in the morning and forget it . . . but I never have.

It was a miracle that Johnny Berry survived the crash. He suffered horrific injuries, so severe that he would never play football again. Born in Aldershot in 1926, he was rejected by his home town club as 'too small to make a footballer', and he left school to become a trainee cinema projectionist. However, his talent for football was recognised by Fred Harris, the Birmingham City captain, who saw him play for his army team in India during the war and brought him to the club when he was demobbed in 1947.

Forty years after the disaster, Johnny Berry's son Neil recalled the crash that nearly killed his father and the tremendous impact it had his family:

> I had just returned home from school and was playing marbles in our street in Davyhulme. My mother shouted loudly for me to come in. Thinking that I was going to get a telling off for something, because I was usually allowed to play out until teatime, and that was still a long way off. But my mother told me that she had just heard on the radio that the plane my father was on had been involved in a crash. I was eight at the time and I thought that this was tremendously exciting news. I imagined him and the other players falling from the sky in parachutes wearing their football kit, much more exciting than being a footballer.
>
> My mother became more and more anxious and within a few minutes some of the other wives and our friends came round to sit and wait for news. It was a night that it is impossible for me to forget and it still lives with me today. Nearly everyone at United was on the plane and there was no ready source of information. We relied totally on the television and radio, and as our communications were much slower in those days we had to wait for hours and hours.
>
> Granada TV gave regular news flashes about the accident, which I still had not fully comprehended. The thought of any of the young men, who had been so good to me as a child, being killed never occurred to me. I still thought that they would fly home on another plane and be ready to play on Saturday. Then the news started coming through. Players' names were given out as being dead or as having survived. This went on throughout the night. My father's name did not come up as being a survivor until six hours after we first heard about the crash. You can

imagine the state we were all in. A Manchester hospital had sent round some nurses, who administered tranquillisers to those who needed them. My mother flew out to Munich the next day, and my brothers and I would not see her or my father for the next three months.

I was sent to school as usual the following morning while arrangements were made for my brothers and me to be looked after. I still had no idea that the events of the previous day were real. My favourite children's television programmes were *Champion the Wonder Horse* and *The Lone Ranger*. The Lone Ranger, especially, was shot at almost every week, fell off his horse and was wounded, but arrived in perfect condition for next week's episode. I felt no real anguish over the crash because my reality consisted of television drama on children's television, where the 'goodies' were never killed. Manchester United were goodies as far as I was concerned. So they were indestructible.

When I arrived at school I was met by a shocked and silent group of children. Not one of them spoke which I found strange; they just stared at me in disbelief. Not being able to comprehend the situation I went up to my teacher, Miss Thornley, and said: 'My dad's been in a plane crash.' 'I know,' she said with tears in her eyes, and took me to the head teacher, Mr Shaw, who asked me how I felt and then asked me to wait outside his room. Everyone who saw me that morning was very kind and I enjoyed the attention, although I was still not sure why I was being treated in this way. At lunchtime I was taken to stay with Harry and Rene MacShane and their son Ian, who went on to become a well known actor of stage and screen. My brothers stayed with family friends until my grandmother and aunt arrived to take us to their home in Folkestone.

Within a week we were put into junior school. It was exceptionally cold in February 1958, but we nevertheless insisted that our aunt took us for a walk every day on the beach with her Pekinese dog. This she did in rain, hail and snow in an attempt to create as normal a life as possible for us in Folkestone at what was obviously a very difficult time.

The true extent of the Munich crash only struck home when I persuaded her to take me to the cinema the following Wednesday and I saw the Pathé newsreel of the crash. I saw pictures of the United party in hospital, including Matt Busby in an oxygen tent, and heard them mention that my father was in a coma. I asked my aunt what this meant, and she told me it meant that he was asleep, which I took to mean that it was night time in Germany.

I now realised that many of the young men who had given me chocolate bars, played football with me and who had always been kind — the likes of Tommy Taylor, Duncan Edwards, Billy Whelan, Roger Byrne and Mark Jones — were now dead. While my mother was in Munich we received regular supplies of German chocolate and at Easter we were sent some special Easter eggs. My aunt did not have a telephone, so we never had the opportunity to speak, and perhaps this was just as well because much later I discovered that my father was not expected to live in the immediate aftermath of the crash and had been given the last rites by a German priest.

Mum told me later that she could scarcely recognise him when she arrived in Munich as his head was swollen to twice its normal size due to the crash impact. He was surrounded by ice to keep the swelling and bruising to a minimum. The nature of my father's injuries were kept from me at the time and I simply thought he was asleep and slightly injured. He was, however, to remain in a coma for almost two months, would never play football again and suffered a complete change in his personality. He went away to play football as one man and returned as a completely different person. He was never able to drive or concentrate for any length of time, and though as he grew older his injuries caused him increasing pain, he seldom complained.

When my parents returned to Manchester from Munich, my father still had no idea what had happened. He thought that he had been in a car crash and knew nothing of the death of his teammates. On the flight back they sat in front of two young male nurses, who had a bag full of tranquillisers in case he had a sudden flashback to the disaster. On his return he was admitted to a hospital in Manchester to help him to continue recovering from his multiple injuries, which included a fractured skull, broken pelvis, and jaw injuries leading to the removal of all his teeth.

We were allowed to see him for the first time in thirteen weeks in May 1958. I remember being very nervous as my brothers and I went into the room. He was, of course, very pleased to see us and made a great fuss of us. It was shortly after this visit that he picked up a newspaper for the first time since the accident and turned to the sports pages. There was a report of a United game and when he saw the team line-up he could not believe it. Where were all his teammates? He asked a nurse and a doctor was brought in to explain what had happened; that was how my father first learned about the crash. Although he had been in the aircraft he must have been the last person in Britain to know about it. He went through the team name by name and the doctor told him whether they were alive or dead. It was very tough for him.

Within a month he had left hospital and began a prolonged period of convalescence. After about a year he began working for a tractor manufacturing firm, who were based in Trafford Park. Shortly afterwards we all moved back to the Aldershot area — my father's home town — where he opened a sports shop with his brother, Peter, a former professional footballer with Ipswich and Crystal Palace. Their partnership lasted for about twenty years and my father eventually finished his working life as a television warehouseman. The Munich air crash changed the life of my family forever. We were all personally traumatised by it, and suffered indescribable private grief.

Chapter 11

Aftermath

Munich wasn't the first time a football team had been decimated in an air crash, nor would it be the last. Nine years earlier, on 4 May 1949, an airliner carrying almost the entire Grande Torino squad — eighteen players plus management, journalists and crew — crashed into the Superga basilica in the hills above Turin, killing all the thirty-one people on board.

The team was returning from a friendly match against Benfica in Lisbon, when their Italian Airlines Fiat G212CP diverted from a planned landing at Milan — for no apparent reason — and made for Turin instead, eighty miles to the north-west. A dense fog enveloped the city and surrounding hills at the time and it seems the pilots decided to descend in search of the airport, with tragic consequences. There was never an official cause of why the plane crashed.

It was the worst disaster in Italian sporting history, since it claimed the lives of a legendary team that had won the Serie A title for the previous four years — plus the last title before the outbreak of war — and were on their way to five when they boarded the plane. The Italian national side that beat Hungary in 1947 contained no fewer than ten Torino players. Only one player survived, Sauro Toma, who did not make the trip because of a knee injury. When he heard the news of the disaster he immediately rushed to Superga in the rain and snow to witness on his arrival hundreds of crying fans streaming down the hill from the crash site. The funeral for the victims attracted an estimated 500,000 people, including supporters from all over Italy and Europe.

There are some amazing parallels between Munich and Superga: like United, their stadium was badly damaged by bombing during the war and rebuilt by a wealthy benefactor (a former Torino player); eight of their players were current internationals, including, like Roger Byrne, their captain Valentino Mazzola; a party of sports journalists travelled with the team on the fatal flight; their coach was an Englishman, Leslie Lievesley, who at one time was on Manchester United's books; and after the disaster, they put out their reserves to complete the rest of the season, as did United.

The Torino club had a long and rich tradition in Italian football but, unlike United, never fully recovered from its misfortune. Overshadowed in the years that followed by its illustrious neighbour Juventus, they yo-yoed between the First and Second Divisions, and they did not win a title again until the 1975–76 season.

The Superga disaster has never been forgotten by the supporters and the people of Turin. On 4 May each year the current Torino team, along with sole survivor Toma and hundreds of supporters, climb the hill of Superga in pilgrimage, to take part in an emotionally charged commemorative ceremony, where the team captain reads out the legendary names of the champions one by one.

It was a heartbroken Jimmy Murphy who returned from Munich with the monumental task of resurrecting Manchester United single-handedly. With his years of work destroyed he knew that the road back was going to be long and hard. Although grief-stricken, Jimmy did his best to keep those left at the club buoyant and positive, but in private he often broke down in tears as he fondly remembered the youngsters he had coached and nurtured to greatness that were now no more.

At first I thought I felt I was going out of my mind, not knowing where to start. Previously Old Trafford had worked like a machine with Matt at the top presiding over all our efforts, sound in judgment and experience, with that incredible flair for public relations, always courteous, urbane and seemingly never forgetting anyone's face, so that he was always able to put people at their ease and talk to them.

But now I had to try and keep the club in business, without Matt's guidance and strength to fall back on, without dear Bert Whalley's unflagging energy and zeal for the club, without Tom Curry, the quiet-spoken yet highly professional team trainer, who also had a lifetime of football experience to draw on. On the administrative side we had lost the club secretary, Walter Crickmer, a man with a shrewd brain which worked with a computer-like efficiency.

With the club's administration in tatters Murphy was fortunate at the time to have Chairman Harold Hardman in charge. Hardman, a dapper little bespectacled man, lived for Manchester United and tenaciously held up their traditions and values. Within days of the disaster he began to reorganise the administrative side of the club. Les Olive, a former United goalkeeper who had made a couple of appearances in the early fifties, was promoted to the post of secretary, replacing Walter Crickmer. Jack Crompton, another goalkeeper, who had played both in the 1948 FA Cup final and the 1952 Championship sides for United, had since retired and was now the trainer at Luton Town. Hardman successfully negotiated with the Luton board to free him from his duties so he could take up the post of first-team trainer left vacant due to Tom Curry's death. All this helped Jimmy Murphy to concentrate all his efforts in putting together some sort of makeshift team and continue as best they could their League, FA Cup and European Cup commitments.

United's game against Wolves on the Saturday following Munich was, under the dreadful circumstances, postponed, but the Football League decreed that the rest of the league fixtures would go ahead. Many of the clubs and their shocked players felt that they

Death in the afternoon: With all hope gone of finding further survivors, the rescue workers face the grim task of recovering the dead. (*Manchester Evening News*)

End of a dream: The true horror of the Munich tragedy is captured in this poignant image that needs no description. (*Manchester Evening News*)

Shroud of snow: In the hours after the crash the weather worsened and continuous heavy snow fell throughout the evening. It was in these conditions that Captain Hans J. Reichel, the chief German accident investigator, claimed to have discovered a layer of ice on the wings. (*News group Newspapers Ltd*)

Traumatic return: The following day Bill Foulkes and Harry Gregg (with his back to the camera and trouser legs rolled up) returned to the scene to search the wreckage for belongings. Amazingly, considering the violence of the crash, Foulkes found an intact bottle of gin which had been given to him at the post-match banquet. (*Manchester Evening News*)

Going home: A BEA Viscount freighter, carrying the coffins of the players, club officials and sports journalists, prepares to leave Munich-Riem Airport bound for Manchester and a sad homecoming. (*Popperfoto/Alamy*)

On the mend: On the road to a full recovery, Matt Busby with his wife Jean, daughter Sheena and nurses at the Rechts der Isar Hospital in Munich. (*Popperfoto/Alamy*)

Memories: Sarah Anne Edwards, seen here in her later years, holds a treasured photograph of her son Duncan, without doubt the greatest footballer of his generation. (*Manchester Evening News*)

Phoenix rising: Captain Bill Foulkes and Jimmy Murphy lead out a makeshift United side at Wembley for the 1958 FA Cup Final. But there was no fairytale ending to that tragic season, with United losing 2–0 to Bolton Wanderers.

Captain James Thain and his wife Ruby at home, look through some of the thousands of pages of documentation that were generated during his eleven-year fight to find justice. (*Thain family archive*)

The Welsh wizard: Relaxing in his Swansea home, Kenny Morgans looks at snapshots of his glory days at Manchester United. He was one of several players badly treated by the club in the aftermath of the disaster. (*Manchester Evening News*)

A photograph of Zulu Uniform taken shortly before taxiing out on its third and fatal take-off attempt, which according to the first German Inquiry shows a layer of snow and ice adhering to the wings. But a careful analysis by British experts ten years later unanimously agreed that the wing was clear of contamination.

The survivors return: At the invitation of UEFA, the surviving Busby Babes returned to Munich for the Champions League final in May 1997. 'As a mark', they said, 'of the enormous contribution they had made to European football.' Left to right: Bill Foulkes, Harry Gregg, Dennis Viollet, Jackie Blanchflower, Bobby Charlton, Ray Wood, Kenny Morgans and Albert Scanlon. (Johnny Berry had died three years earlier.) (*Popperfoto/Alamy*)

Like father like son: Steve Rayment followed in his father's footsteps and became a pilot. Based in the Middle East, he is a captain on Gulfstream Executive jets. Steve is seen here at the Munich Air Disaster Memorial near the village of Kirchtudering. (*Steve Rayment*)

should not have been asked play so soon after the disaster. At three o'clock football grounds up and down the country, with their flags at half mast, were hushed as supporters and players alike, wearing black armbands, stood with heads bowed as referees indicated a period of two minutes' silence by a blast on their whistles.

United's fifth-round FA Cup tie against Sheffield Wednesday had also been postponed from Saturday 15 February until the following Wednesday evening. Murphy, now working eighteen hours a day every day and often sleeping overnight in his office, knew he had to field a team by that date or opt out of the competition altogether. He still had a wealth of talented youngsters at the club, and although they had basic ability they lacked first-team experience. So in desperation he cast around for new players to augment his depleted squad. But many of those he wanted to sign were either unavailable or too expensive. There were even rumours flying around at the time that United were trying to recruit Hungary's legendary 'Galloping Major' Ferenc Puskas, but in the end it came to nothing.

Murphy was in desperate need of an experienced inside-forward and negotiations were opened with Blackpool for the transfer of Ernie Taylor for £8,000. Taylor was at the end of his career and many felt he was past his best. At 5 feet 4 inches and only 9 stone he looked as if he had just got up from his sick bed. But he was a cunning and skilful player with the ability to open up the opponents' defence with just a single pass. In those dark weeks and months after Munich, Ernie Taylor inspired the United players to greater heights. He once said to Bobby Charlton in a match, 'When I look up, all I want to see is your arse disappearing up the field. Give me something to aim at.'

In preparation for the game against Sheffield Wednesday, Murphy took his players off to the comparative calm of Norbreck Hydro Hotel in Blackpool for a week-long break away from the mourning gloom of Manchester. There they trained each day on the beach, took long walks in the fresh air and readied themselves for an emotional return to Old Trafford. For the inexperienced youngsters the tragedy affected them deeply — they all knew they shouldered the heavy burden to haul United back from out of the shadows.

Shay Brennan was one of them. Despite being an FA Youth Cup winner in 1955, playing alongside Duncan Edwards, Mark Jones and Eddie Colman, he remained in their shadow as they were elevated to the first team. He thought he stood no chance of being selected for the game; however, at 10.30 on the morning of the match he got a call at the hotel from Jimmy Murphy. He was flabbergasted when he told him that he would be making his senior debut in Albert Scanlon's number eleven shirt on the left wing. For Brennan it was the first step in a glittering Old Trafford career that would bring him 355 first-team appearances, two League Championship winner's medals and the European Cup triumph at Wembley in 1968. Many years later the Republic of Ireland international admitted that if it hadn't been for Munich he'd never have made the grade at Old Trafford. 'I'll never forget that so many friends and a great team died to enable that to happen.'

Murphy chose Colin Webster to fill outside-right position. He had made his debut in the 1953–54 season and won a League Championship medal in 1956 after making fifteen appearances, but was then edged out of the side by Johnny Berry. At inside-left was Mark Pearson, nicknamed 'Pancho' by the fans because of the Mexican appearance his long sideburns gave him. He was a powerful player and regular goal scorer with the lower sides. Leading the team at centre-forward was Alex Dawson, a brawny Scot who had made his debut as a sixteen-year-old in April 1957, scoring against Burnley.

On the day of the match the fans converged on Old Trafford in their thousands and extra police had to be called in to control the thronging masses. Everyone in Manchester and beyond desperately wanted to see the game and there was a mad scramble for tickets. Touts, some of whom had travelled all the way from London, did a roaring trade selling tickets for vastly inflated prices. The stadium was soon packed to capacity and the gates were locked two hours before the scheduled kick-off time, leaving thousands of spectators standing disappointed outside in the cold.

On the packed terraces and stands the fans, wearing red and white scarves, draped in black, wept openly — they all knew this was going to be a night of tears and memories. In that emotional atmosphere, which verged on near hysteria, the Sheffield players knew they stood no chance. They would rather be anywhere else than Old Trafford that night. Albert Quixall, the Wednesday skipper — soon to join United in a record-breaking deal — who knew many of the Babes from his international, army and schoolboy days, said, 'There was no way Sheffield Wednesday could have won, the whole country was behind United and I suspect so were the rest of my side. I led my team down the tunnel after United. Never could the emotion of that evening have hit anyone harder.'

On the front of the sombre match programme the bold headline proclaimed 'United Will Go On'. It also contained a poignant tribute to all those who had been killed and injured in the tragedy. The team sheet was symbolically left blank and the fans were told to write in the names of the players. Few did. They listened in silence as the United team was announced over the speakers: Gregg, Foulkes, Greaves, Goodwin, Cope, Crowther, Webster, Taylor, Dawson, Pearson, Brennan. Only Foulkes and Gregg linked the pre-Munich side; the other names and faces were not so familiar, and for those who cared to look the same was true in the press box.

Both Gregg and Foulkes should never have been asked to play so soon after the trauma of Munich, but out of loyalty to Murphy they wanted to do all they could to help United out of the desperate crisis they were in. Bill Foulkes, now appointed captain, said, 'Everything was getting too much for me and, in all honesty, the last thing I wanted to do was to play football. I wasn't eating or sleeping properly and I was losing weight rapidly. I guess I was teetering on the brink of some sort of breakdown, but had no appreciation of that at the time.' A few days after his return from Munich Bill Foulkes, with a heavy heart, took over Roger Byrne's weekly column in the *Manchester Evening News*. He wrote: 'When I was young I used dream of captaining a great side like Manchester United. Now my dream has come true, but I wish it hadn't.'

Harry Gregg, like Foulkes, not only suffered from the mental anguish of Munich but physically as well, from an undiagnosed injury. Soon after the accident he began to suffer from severe headaches and bouts of dizziness. It was only later after he had been examined by a neurosurgeon that it was discovered he had fractured his skull in the crash. That was kept a closely guarded secret, Gregg preferring to suffer in silence until he had recovered.

Playing at left-half for United was Stan Crowther, the Aston Villa player who played against United in the controversial 1957 Cup final. The fact that he turned out for the Reds that evening was remarkable. Jimmy Murphy recalls: 'Eric Houghton was the Villa manager at the time and he had told Stan that we were interested in him. He didn't want to leave Villa, but Eric got him to come to Old Trafford to watch the Sheffield Wednesday game. On the way up he told him he thought that he should help us out, but Stan told him he hadn't brought any kit with him. "Don't worry, I've got your boots in my bag," Eric said. We met at about half-past five and an hour before the kick-off he'd signed!'

Just thirteen days after the disaster, football returned to Old Trafford. In the dressing room the players, lost in their own thoughts, changed in silence — there was none of the laughing and joking that usually preceded a game. At left full-back was Ian Greaves; although he had won a championship medal in the 1955–56 season, he had played most of his football in the reserves. Suddenly he found himself catapulted into the first team, replacing Roger Byrne. 'I can remember the dressing room was very quiet,' he said. 'I couldn't get Roger out of my mind; I was getting changed where he would have sat. I was wearing his shirt . . .'

It was a pale and sombre-faced Bill Foulkes who emerged out of the players' tunnel to lead the makeshift United team onto the floodlit Old Trafford pitch to a deafening wall of sound from the 60,000 emotionally charged fans. Shay Brennan, the twenty-year-old novice was first to score direct from a corner — Albert Quixall was convinced the crowd blew it in! He later got a second when a shot from Mark Pearson rebounded off the keeper straight to his feet; he made no mistake and slammed the ball home into the back of the net to put United two up. Five minutes from the end of that incredible game Alex Dawson scored the third to put them through to the quarter-finals of the FA Cup. There was no doubt in anyone's mind that it was the sheer emotion and passion that cascaded down from the terraces that swept United to victory that night.

When the final whistle blew, the fans, with outstretched arms, exploded with a roar that reverberated for miles around the ground. They had just seen out of the ashes the resurrection of Manchester United. Albert Quixall recalled: 'I don't think anyone who played in the game or watched it will ever forget that night. United ran their hearts out, and no matter how well we had played they would have beaten us. They were playing like men inspired. We were playing more than just eleven players; we were playing 60,000 fans as well.'

The *Manchester Guardian* reported: 'As the triumphant crowds swept homeward, whole families stood on their doorsteps in sombre little streets — including sleepless children in their pyjamas, mothers with their hair in curling pins — all asking, "Who won? Who scored? What were they like?" over and over again, until they were convinced that Old Trafford was back in the business it knows so well.'

The horror of Munich was far from over. Two days after that historic Cup tie, in the early hours of the morning, Duncan Edwards, the greatest footballer of his generation, lost his fight for life and died in the Rechts der Isar Hospital. He was just twenty-one and had not even reached his peak. Since the crash he had fought with the same courage he had shown on the football field. English football would never see his likes again. If the doctors and surgeons had somehow miraculously managed to save him he would probably have spent the rest of his life in a wheelchair, a pitiful caricature of his former self. Duncan would certainly not have wanted that. Perhaps it was better this way and he is remembered as he was in his zenith.

Many years later Bobby Charlton paid this tribute to his teammate: 'The best player that I've ever seen, the best footballer that I've ever played with for United or England, and the only player who ever made me feel inferior.'

After being discharged from the Rechts der Isar Hospital in

Munich, Bobby Charlton returned to his home in Ashington, County Durham, where he spent his time moping about. His mother Cissie was concerned about him and made an appointment with Dr McPherson, the family GP. McPherson had been in the RAF during the war and had seen at first hand the effects of aircraft accidents on his friends. After a long talk with Bobby he told him the best advice he could give him was to get back to playing football as soon as possible. A few days later Bobby phoned Jimmy Murphy at Old Trafford and told him he was coming back. Murphy was delighted; he desperately needed him to bolster the threadbare team. He tried him out in a hastily arranged practice match at Old Trafford behind closed doors and, impressed with his performance, told him he would be playing in the sixth-round FA Cup tie against West Bromwich Albion.

West Brom was one of the strongest teams in the First Division in those days with the legendary Don Howe and future England manager Bobby Robson in the side, and on paper should have had little difficulty in disposing of an under-strength United. Their manager, Vic Buckingham, told the press before the game that although his team had sympathy for United's predicament, they were determined to knock them out of the competition, but Murphy's patched-up side, playing in memory of the Babes, had other ideas.

In front of 60,000 spectators at the Hawthorns, the game got underway with United taking the game straight to the Baggies, causing them to panic and make mistakes. The diminutive Ernie Taylor played his heart out and inside six minutes he had the ball in the back of the net, only for West Brom to equalise a few minutes later. Then just before the interval a blistering shot from Taylor rattled the crossbar, leaving Alex Dawson to race in and head home the rebound to put United ahead. After the interval West Brom piled on the pressure that saw Harry Gregg, for the last twenty minutes of the game, fearlessly throw himself around his goal to thwart the fierce onslaught from their forwards. Then, with four minutes left on the clock, Roy Horobin scored a controversial equaliser; those watching were convinced that Ronnie Cope had cleared the ball before it crossed the line. It was cruel goal that denied United a well-deserved victory.

The replay took place under the floodlights of Old Trafford the following Wednesday in front of 60,000 screaming fans with an estimated 40,000 locked outside when the gates were closed. From the start West Brom mercilessly pressured United for the whole game and on their performance deserved to win. But in the final minute, with normal time running out and extra time looming, Bobby Charlton from the right wing set off on a devastating run, weaving past man after man before squaring the ball to Colin Webster, who calmly side-footed the ball over the goal line. The game was won. Old Trafford erupted in an ear-splitting explosion of noise with scarves, hats, programmes and anything else to hand thrown into the air by the rapturous jigging fans. It is said that the noise rattled the windows of nearby houses and could be heard three miles away. It was an unforgettable end to an unforgettable game of football.

Three days later United faced West Bromwich for the third time, on this occasion for a League match at Old Trafford. Attending the game was Professor Georg Maurer and a party of doctors and nurses from the Rechts der Isar Hospital in Munich. They were invited by the City of Manchester and the club in appreciation of their tireless work in treating and caring for the victims of the disaster.

Before the game they attended a civic reception at Stretford Town Hall, a stone's throw from Old Trafford. After the formalities were completed in the mayor's parlour, Professor Maurer responded to the enthusiastic chanting crowd that had gathered outside by going onto the balcony and giving them messages from the players still in hospital. He told them, 'They came to us as badly injured patients but, step by step, they have become our friends. We know what Manchester United means to England and especially to Manchester. We will do all in our power to send back the brilliant lads who are so dear to your hearts.'

Before the kick-off many a tear was shed by the fans when a tape recording made by Matt Busby from his hospital bed was played to the hushed crowd:

Ladies and gentlemen, I am speaking from my bed in the Isar

Hospital in Munich, where I been for a month since the tragic accident. You will be glad I'm sure, that the remaining players here, and myself, are now considered out of danger and this can be attributed to the wonderful treatment given us by Professor Maurer and his staff, who are with you today as guests of the club.

It is only in the past two or three days that I have been able to be told about football and I am delighted to hear of the success and united effort made by all at Old Trafford. Again it is wonderful to hear that the club has reached the semi-final of the FA Cup and I extend my best wishes to everyone.

With that, the United Chairman Harold Hardman led Professor Maurer and his party — now dubbed 'The Angels of Munich' — out through the players' tunnel onto the pitch to the thunderous applause of 60,000 appreciative fans; Maurer and his team were clearly taken aback by the rapturous reception and waved back in response before taking their seats in the stand.

The game itself was a disappointment, with United going down 4–0. The defeat summed up United's abysmal performance in the League, recording only a single win between the accident and the season's end. But incredibly, in the FA Cup they defied all the odds to reach the final after beating Fulham 5–3 in a classic semi-final replay at Highbury.

For a month after the accident Matt Busby lay in the Rechts der Isar Hospital recovering from his life-threatening injuries, protected by a wall of silence from the truth about the terrible losses that had decimated his precious Babes. When he was well enough it was left to his wife, Jean, to reveal the worst. Busby recalled: 'I came to one day and Jean was there, leaning over me. I said, "What happened?" She said nothing, so I went through the names of the players. She didn't even look at me as she said, "Dead ... dead ... dead ... dead ..." To be honest, I suppose I wasn't sane. I wanted to die. I felt that, in a way, I might have been responsible, for allowing us to go the third time. What was so special about me that I'd survived? I was absolutely determined that I'd have nothing more to do with football.'

When he was discharged from hospital on crutches he went to Interlaken in Switzerland for a long period of convalescence. It was while he was there that Jean casually said to him one day, 'You know Matt, the lads would have wanted you to carry on.' With those words the black depression lifted and his enthusiasm for the game was suddenly rekindled. A few days later he travelled back home by train and ferry in time to see United face Bolton Wanderers in the FA Cup final.

Before Busby took his seat as a spectator in the Wembley stands with the United officials, he managed to hobble on his crutches into the dressing room to wish the boys luck. Murphy and the players, who were now being dubbed Murphy's Marvels by the press, wanted him to lead the team out, but Busby insisted that Jimmy must do it, being the man who had brought them so far. Jimmy told his players before they left the dressing room, 'Lads, to get this far has been a miracle. I would just like to say a big thank you from the bottom of my heart for all you have done. Win, lose or draw, I am proud of each and every one of you.'

Jimmy Murphy's Cup final team read: Gregg, Foulkes, Greaves, Goodwin, Cope, Crowther, Dawson, Taylor, Charlton, Viollet and Webster. Jimmy proudly led his team out through the tunnel onto the manicured Wembley turf bathed in the bright May sunshine. Emblazoned on their red shirts was a new badge depicting a phoenix rising from the ashes; it said everything that anyone needed to know about Murphy's post-Munich side.

But there was no fairy-tale ending to that tragic season. Something strange happened to United that day; it seemed as if the whole trauma of Munich had suddenly caught up with them. Inside five minutes Bolton opened the scoring with a low drive from Nat Lofthouse that Harry Gregg had no chance of saving. Against the run of play Bobby Charlton came close when one of his trademark cannonball shots rattled the post with the Bolton keeper beaten. Minutes later Nat Lofthouse put the Wanderers two up with a controversial goal that should have been disallowed. A high cross from Dennis Stevens had Gregg leaping up to catch the ball when the onrushing Lofthouse steamrollered Gregg and the ball over the line. The United players were convinced it was a foul and were dumbfounded when Sherlock, the referee, awarded the goal. It was a cruel decision that handed Bolton the cup. But if the truth be told Wanderers were the better team on the day. A furious Harry Gregg said, 'Nat blatantly barged me over the line, a goal should never had been awarded. I remember sitting seething in the bath at Wembley praying that Lofthouse wouldn't retire before I had had a chance to get my own back. I am happy to tell you that he didn't . . . and I did!'

After the match Nat Lofthouse came clean and admitted that his controversial goal should never have been allowed:

> I am quite convinced that I did foul Gregg, but you could hardly expect me to argue when the referee gave the goal. Even so, I believe we deserved to win. United never put us under pressure. We always seemed to have something in hand. It was an emotional occasion when the final whistle blew, but what really left me with a lump in my throat was when Matt Busby, supported by walking sticks, limped into our dressing room after the match to congratulate us. What a magnificent gesture.

Three months had now passed since the disaster and United were obliged to fulfil their European Cup semi-final commitment. On 8 May the Reds ran out at Old Trafford to face the mighty AC Milan in the first leg. Four of the surviving Babes lined up in the team — Bill Foulkes, Harry Gregg, Dennis Viollet and Kenny Morgans. Bobby Charlton should have made it five, but the FA had unbelievably called him up to play for England in a meaningless friendly game against Portugal at Wembley, so his place was taken by Ernie Taylor. Surprisingly, and against all the odds, United won the game 2–1 with a goal from Dennis Viollet and a penalty from Taylor.

When United arrived in Italy six days later to face Milan in the second leg, any post-Munich sympathy had disappeared as the United players were bombarded with vegetables from 80,000 hostile fans when they ran out into the San Siro stadium. Bill Foulkes recalled: 'I remember being struck by a shower of cabbages and the biggest bunch of carrots I have ever seen.' With flares and fireworks adding to the hostility it came as no surprise that Milan outplayed United and triumphed with a 4–0 victory.

That ended Manchester United's 1957–58 European Cup campaign — a sad end to a tragic season. They were invited, as a mark of respect for the players who lost their lives, to take part in the competition the following season. But the Football League, still resentful after Busby flouted their authority a few years earlier, made sure by every means at their disposal to deny United the opportunity. With that Busby had no choice but to bow out of the competition and concentrate all his efforts on rebuilding the team. He had no doubts whatsoever that Manchester United would rise from the ashes of Munich to one day become European Champions.

Chapter 12

Scapegoat

The West German inquiry into the Munich air disaster opened on the morning of Tuesday 28 April 1958 in the conference room at Munich-Riem Airport, chaired by Judge Walter Stimpel, a former Luftwaffe pilot who would conduct the proceedings. The other members of the Commission were Hans Reichel, the chief investigator; Professor Gunter Bock, an aviation expert; and Captain Werner Utter, a pilot with Lufthansa.

Besides Thain, the British contingent included: Henry Marking, the BEA secretary; Captain Poole, the Elizabethan flight manager; J. W. Gibbs, the chief accident investigator; and J. R. D. Kenward, from the Performance and Analysis section. Also in the British group were Captains Gilman and Key; although employees of BEA they came along as representatives of Thain's union, BALPA. G. M. Kelly, the accredited UK representative, brought with him R. F. Jones, a meteorological expert.

The inquiry room was dominated by a long table where the interested parties faced each other and a glass booth was provided for the interpreter. Although armed guards were on duty outside, the general atmosphere within the room was, according to Thain, 'friendly'.

In his opening speech, Stimpel welcomed everyone present and said:

I think I can assure all those who were personally involved in the events of 6 February, especially Captain Thain and the gentlemen from BEA, that the members of this Commission feel a close relationship with them, and will try to carry out this investigation objectively and in accordance with our duty, of course, but also with a deep interest and understanding of your personal fate.

The object of this inquiry is to extend the frontiers of knowledge, and serve aviation as a whole. We want to learn from it for the future, and we can only do so by examining and discussing this accident together. I am sure, gentlemen, that you will help us to conduct the inquiry in this spirit.

It seemed from Stimpel's opening remarks that the inquiry would be administered in fairness and with the sole object of discovering the causes of why Zulu Uniform had crashed, and hopefully prevent another accident in similar circumstances. But as the inquiry progressed, it soon became clear to Thain and the British contingent that some of those present were intent on diverting the course of the inquiry into murky waters far away from the truth.

After his opening address, Stimpel called on Reichel, as the chief investigator, to formally open the inquiry. He began by reading out his own report of his investigation and detailed the familiar events leading up to the third and final take-off attempt and subsequent accident. He then turned to the evidence found on the ground taken in part from a written statement by Reinhardt Meyer, the first person to arrive on the crash scene:

The wheel tracks from this third attempt were clearly visible at the end of the 1,907 metre runway and beyond it in the slush. This showed that the aircraft did not become airborne at any time. This was confirmed by most of the witnesses' statements. Just short of the end of the runway the emergency tailwheel is said to have left a clearly visible track for quite a long distance. I myself did not see this track, since numerous aircraft used the runway during the interval before my arrival. The track was however clearly preserved at the end of the runway and on the 250 metre stopway beyond it, as far as the fence which encloses the airport grounds. The tracks of the left-hand wheels were visible only sporadically as far as the fence. The tracks of the twin wheels on the right hand side of the undercarriage had made a continuous and firm impression. There was no sign of a nosewheel track.

The emergency tailwheel was so situated to prevent damage to the rear of the fuselage when the aircraft is at extreme nose-up attitude during take-off. The impression it made on the ground clearly demonstrates the high nose-up angle Rayment forced on the aircraft in his vain effort to get airborne.

Reichel then moved on to his examination of the wreckage on his arrival at 10.00 p.m., and his subsequent discovery of a layer of ice on the wings. He went to great pains to point out to those listening that, with the exception of Zulu Uniform, all other aircraft at Munich that afternoon had been de-iced before departure. This last point was no doubt directly aimed at Thain and the British party.

He concluded his evidence with a description of the runway conditions on the day of the accident:

There were varying opinions on the snow conditions on the runway. The quantity of snow which had fallen up to the time of the third attempted take-off would be about four centimetres. However, the snow had fallen on a non-frozen and very wet base, so that it had subsided to form a layer of slush. At the time of my landing at 22.00 hours it was snowing relatively heavily. The landing was carried out in the east-west direction, i.e. in the take-off direction of G-ALZU. Our comparatively light aircraft equipped with nosewheel landing gear rolled unimpeded by the snow right up to the end of the runway, up to that time no snow had been cleared from the runway.

So far Reichel's presentation of the evidence was so biased that it left no one in any doubt where his personal opinion lay, an

opinion he confidently believed the Commission would agree with
— that ice on the wings, caused by Thain's failure to have the
aircraft de-iced before departure, was the decisive factor. The
whole point of the inquiry was to establish the cause of the
accident, not to put any individual on trial, yet here was Thain
from the very start up against the ropes and very much on the
defensive.

According to German regulations, Thain would not normally be
allowed to participate in the proceedings, but in this instance he
was invited out of courtesy. He had no rights to produce his own
witnesses to support his own theories and no legal representation.
All those in his party were merely there to advise him. He had no
knowledge of who the witnesses would be, or what they would say.
Thain felt, quite rightly, that he would stand a better chance in a
court of law.

After Reichel had completed his evidence, Stimpel invited Thain
to the vacant chair in front of him to read his statement. Apart
from one or two interruptions from Stimpel to clarify a point here
and there he was heard in silence. Thain described in detail the
events of 6 February and concluded with his attempts to
extinguish the fires around the wreckage and the rescue
operations. He was followed by the first witness, Siegfried
Schombel.

Schombel was a nineteen-year-old air navigation trainee at
Munich Airport. He had previously spent three years at Hamburg
Airport on apron service and had experience in de-icing aircraft.
On the day of the accident he claimed to have seen from the
airport building a layer of snow on the wing of Zulu Uniform
shortly before it taxied out on the third take-off attempt. He told
the Commission:

> I was able to see the upper surface of the aircraft plainly from
> the second floor of the main building from a distance of not
> more than fifty metres. In spite of the propeller slipstream, the
> snow remained on the wing.
>
> I told my colleagues that I was surprised that the aircraft was
> not de-iced before take-off. After the mechanic had given the 'all

clear' signal for taxiing the snow remained lying on the wings, it was sticky, wet snow.

I was able to observe in detail the course of events from the beginning of the attempted take-off until the accident. It struck me that, approximately from halfway along the runway, the pilot was trying, with all his might, to get the aircraft off the ground, and I noticed the particularly large angle of attack. The nosewheel was high in the air, the emergency tailwheel, according to my observation, was on the ground. I was not able to observe the actual impact at the scene of the accident.

The Commission now returned to the written evidence of Reinhardt Meyer, the first person on the scene, and his observations of the wheel tracks. Reichel told the Commission that he had invited Meyer to appear as a witness but unfortunately he was unable to attend, but Meyer had sent him a copy of his report — the same report that Reichel had read out earlier detailing the wheel markings on the ground. This statement from Reichel was blatantly untrue, as we will discover later. Meyer, an aeronautical engineer and qualified pilot who would have made an expert witness, was deliberately not called by Reichel to give evidence. Also, vital information included in his original written report had been deliberately removed.

The next witness to give evidence was Robert Wiggers, who worked for BP and was one of those who had refuelled Zulu Uniform soon after its arrival at Munich. He said: 'Refuelling took place in driving snow. I noticed that the inner section of the wing was clear of snow, whereas there was snow lying on the outer section. I cannot testify as to whether there was still snow on the wings when the aircraft returned from the abortive take-off attempts.'

Under questioning from Stimpel, Wiggers added that as he stood on the wing to direct the refuelling, 'the inner part of the wing was wet during the filling, which means that the snow, which was falling heavily at that time, melted at once. It was watery, not slush.'

The Commission then shifted its attention away from the

weather conditions to the house situated at the end of the runway, which certainly contributed to the seriousness of the accident. An expert on airport construction, Carl Gerlach, gave a long discourse on the regulations on the location of such buildings on or near airfields. He said as the house in question existed before the airport was constructed and approved, it was designated an obstruction and was fitted with double obstruction lights, and therefore, according to Gerlach, did not contravene either German or international aviation regulations. But there can be no doubt that if the house had not been in the path of Zulu Uniform when it left the runway, most of the passengers would have been able to walk away from the crash with only minor injuries. It is interesting to note that permission to reconstruct the wrecked building was denied and the remains were demolished shortly after.

Next to take the hot seat was Bill Black, the BEA station engineer. He quoted from his original statement, giving his account of the two abandoned take-offs and his subsequent discussion on the flight deck with Thain and Rayment about the boost surging. There were no surprises here, but when he described the final attempt to take off, things began to get bit confused. Black, who watched the third take-off attempt from the top of the steps of another aircraft that had recently landed, said he had the impression that the aircraft's attitude was very steep during the final part of the run, but was unsure if the emergency tailwheel had touched the runway, because of the amount of spray coming from the nose of the aircraft. The Commission were somewhat mystified by this comment. 'How', they asked, 'could so much spray come up in front of the main wheels, if the nosewheel is in the air?' The Commission went around in ever decreasing circles trying to find a plausible explanation for Black's observation and in the end came to the conclusion that he was mistaken by what he saw due to the great distance from which his observation was made.

Stimpel then deliberately steered the discussion away from the subject with a most telling remark: 'I think we will keep this question in mind so that we can come back to it if necessary. *I'm afraid we are getting too far away from the question of ice.*' Ice again, it seemed, was at the forefront of this inquiry and Stimpel for one was not going to let it go. He pursued the subject with the BEA engineer:

> Stimpel: *After the second attempt to take off, and before the third attempt, did you speak to either of the captains about ice, and can you remember whether, after the second attempt, you took another look at the surface of the wings?*
>
> Black: *Prior to the last take-off, after I had talked to Captains Thain and Rayment, I walked round the aircraft on the ground, observing as much of the main plane as possible. There was only a very light covering of snow on the wing tips.*

Professor Gunter Bock, the German aviation expert, then said to no one in particular, 'I think it would be interesting to hear how much of the surface of the wing can be observed from the ground.' Bill Black, knowing that this statement was aimed at him, said, 'You can see a reasonable portion of the wing, depending on how far back you are from the aircraft.'

There were no further questions and with that Black left the chair. During the short delay before the next witness was called Reichel, eager to promote his 'ice on the wings' theory, took the opportunity to pass around a photograph of Zulu Uniform. It was taken from the airport building shortly before it taxied out on the third and final take-off attempt, and it showed, according to Reichel, snow or ice obscuring the lettering and markings on the top surface of the wings.

The next witness was Count zu Castell, the Director of Munich-Riem Airport. He had arrived at the crash scene soon after the emergency services and decided to trace the aircraft wheel tracks back towards the runway.

> Here I found to my surprise that the tracks led up to the road, to the fence which encloses the airport. I realised then that the plane had never taken off, and that something must have hindered it from lifting off. The weather conditions suggested that probably ice was involved. Meanwhile the undamaged right wing — this was about an hour after the accident — was

covered with more snow, and I could see no sign that anyone had touched it. So I decided not to disturb it myself, so that the experts examining the case would have an untouched surface to work on.

His decision not to check the surface of the wings was highly unfortunate. Six hours were to elapse before the 'expert' — in this case Reichel — arrived at the scene and discovered what he and everyone else expected to see: ice.

Castell then went on to describe his late-night excursion to the crash site with Reichel shortly after his arrival and the examination of the wings.

Herr Reichel and myself established the fact that the surface was completely untouched because the snow cover was completely even. During our examination, on many parts of the surface, we quite definitely felt and saw a rough course-grained layer of ice on the surface of the wing. The nose of the wing (leading edge) was free of ice; the engine nacelle and the area of the wing behind it were also free of ice though covered with snow. I should like to add that there was ice on some parts of the airscrews. The rough layer of ice on the wing would have been five millimetres at the least, if not thicker.

How Castell arrived at the thickness of 5 millimetres without any means of accurately measuring it was not queried. But ice on the propellers was. If ice could form there after the crash then the same was true for the wing. Kenward, the BEA engineer, asked Castell whether he had actually seen ice on the wing or just felt it. 'I could recognise the ice on the surface absolutely clearly with the eye,' replied Castell. 'But since I examined so many points on the wing I had to rely mainly on feeling, having definitely recognised ice optically at some points.'

Kelly, the UK representative, pointed out to the Commission that all these observations took place in driving snow and in darkness without adequate lighting. He asked Stimpel, 'Did any one carry out any examination of any kind immediately after the accident?'

Stimpel replied, 'No, we have nothing.' Stimpel believed this to be true beyond doubt, but he along with everyone else had been deliberately misinformed by Reichel. There was, in fact, one person who had checked the wing minutes after the accident and found no ice. Reichel, who hand-picked the witnesses, knew this and because it contradicted his own theory deliberately kept him out of the loop.

With that the first day of the inquiry came to an end, with the Commission seemingly accepting that ice on the wing had been established beyond doubt.

The second day began with the testimony of Dr Muller from a nearby meteorological station. He stated: 'As a meteorologist, one cannot completely exclude the possibility that in the six hours between the accident and the observation of a layer of ice, a certain irregular layer of ice could have formed on certain parts of the plane.' But his opinion failed to explain the ice-free areas discovered behind the engine nacelles — the most likely place for icing to form.

Dr Schlichting, a professor of stream mechanics at Brunswick University, was then invited to give evidence on the aerodynamic effects of icing on the wings. He considered that if the amount of ice found six hours after the accident was present on the final run, it would make take-off impossible, but he was unable to demonstrate, aerodynamically, the retardation of speed experienced by Captain Thain.

Even though there were more witnesses to be called and other aspects of the accident still to be examined, Stimpel made the following pronouncement, which clearly indicated that the Germans had already made up their minds as to the cause: 'Unless, today or tomorrow,' he said, 'we find a different cause of the accident — which is unlikely — then we must meet again in a few weeks' time to discuss these questions in detail.' Ice, as far as the Commission was concerned, was the culprit, and the only thing left for the inquiry to do now was to make the discrepancies in the evidence fit the theory.

One explanation why Zulu Uniform lost speed at the end of the take-off run was the depth of undisturbed slush on the last third of the runway. This was of great interest to Thain, who from the very beginning believed that it was this that retarded his aircraft sufficiently from attaining flying speed.

Kurt Bartz was the only witness called to give evidence regarding the state of the runway on the afternoon of the accident. As the Munich Airport technical manager, he was responsible for observing the surface conditions and reporting the information back to the airport authority. With the expected arrival of the West German Chancellor, the airport director was anxious to have the runway checked. Bartz, with his deputy, were dispatched and drove out to wait at the edge of the eastern end of the runway from where they watched Zulu Uniform make its second attempt to take off. After it was aborted they waited until the aircraft taxied to the end of the runway and left via the perimeter track on its way back to the terminal. This left the way clear for Bartz to enter the runway and travel its full length to carry out the inspection. He told the Commission:

> We drove on to the runway and left the car to have a look at the conditions. We found the whole runway covered in slush, about half to three quarters of a centimetre deep. It was not snow, but a watery, gelatinous mass. We stopped several times and noticed that the tracks left from the first two take-off attempts were pure water.
>
> Herr Meyer and I both left the car, twice, to measure the depth of slush. The inspection took perhaps three to four minutes. We began at the eastern end and left the runway at the western end, returning to the airport building. On my way from the hall to my office I saw the take-off which led to the accident.

The most astonishing part of Bartz's evidence is the timing. Considering the runway at Munich is just over a mile long and he travelled the whole length, stopping at least twice to measure the depth of slush, and the fact that he estimates the whole exercise took four minutes at the most, it points to a cursory check at best, and the use of a Volkswagen with the performance of a sports car!

The last witness to be called on the second day was Kenward, the

BEA performance and analysis engineer. He had been involved with the Elizabethan since it was introduced into BEA service in 1952. In the interval between the accident and the inquiry he had written a number of papers on the aerodynamic characteristics of the aircraft. According to his calculations, up to 3 inches of ice adhering to the wings of Zulu Uniform would have been needed to cause any noticeable difference to the lifting properties of the wing. Reichel's measurement of 5 millimetres (one-fifth of an inch) therefore would have made no difference at all. This evidence also flew in the face of Schlichting, who stated earlier that with a layer of 5 millimetres of ice on the wings take-off would be impossible.

Kenward also introduced evidence regarding the acceleration characteristics of the Elizabethan. He said that even with a thick layer of ice on the wings it was insufficient to account for the drop in speed after reaching V1. In attempting to explain the deceleration, he pointed out that slush on the runway could have played a far greater role than had been previously appreciated, but admitted that 'nobody knows much about it'.

The third and final day began with a discussion on the roles the pilots played in the cockpit on the day of the crash. Stimpel asked about the relationship between the commander and the co-pilot, and who had the responsibility, especially during take-off. What happens when the commander leaves the take-off to the co-pilot, and who makes the decisions when the take-off has to be abandoned? Could any misunderstanding have occurred between the two, with one attempting to take off, the other trying to abort? And why was Thain, as commander, sitting in the right-hand seat? It fell to Captain Poole, manager of the Elizabethan flight, to try and clarify the situation on the flight deck, but in the end his interpretation left the Commission even more confused.

At this point, Henry Marking for BEA produced the airline staff instruction document that requires the captain of the aircraft to always to sit in the left-hand seat. Thain was furious. Why had Marking, who was supposedly on his side, chosen to impart this information to the Commission? It had no bearing whatsoever on the accident. By swapping seats he had not broken any national or international aviation law, and the seating arrangement was purely a private matter between the airline and himself. Later Thain asked him why he had done it. Marking just shrugged his shoulders and said, 'I felt I had to.' Thain was convinced that the decision to bring up the instruction came from higher up in the echelons of BEA.

At the end of the last day Thain managed to introduce the KLM flight manual issued to its crews, warning of the dangers of attempting to take off in slush. Stimpel read out the relevant parts to the Commission with little conviction, and with that he called an adjournment until further notice.

The inquiry was resumed on 25 June, this time in the conference room of the Federal Bureau for Air Safety in Frankfurt. Time and further investigation had not changed the Germans' stance that ice was the major factor in causing the accident. The same views from both sides were reiterated apart from some new evidence from the British meteorologist, Mr R. Jones, in support for Thain. He calculated that in order for a layer of ice 5 millimetres thick to form on the wing, 4 to 5 centimetres of snow would have to fall and melt. Since it had been established beyond doubt that only half a centimetre of snow fell while Zulu Uniform was on the ground at Munich, where had all this extra snow come from? No one asked. The Germans simply didn't want to know, because this evidence theoretically blew their whole case out of the water.

Kenward, the BEA performance expert, had also come up with some interesting conclusions. He advanced the theory he first touched upon in Munich in April, that of the slush factor. He suggested to the Commission that if slush drag was related to speed, not weight, as the German expert contended, then a very different picture emerged. On a blackboard he drew a graph that plotted drag against speed; the resulting curve clearly demonstrated that on a runway covered with a layer of slush, not only could acceleration be retarded, but deceleration could also take place. Exactly what Thain had experienced on that final take-off attempt.

But whatever new evidence was put before the Germans, it seemed to fall on deaf ears. After an adjournment for lunch the parties reassembled to hear Stimpel give an interim verdict which the Commission had reached:

> When the aircraft landed at Munich it had been severely super-cooled at great height. During the time it stayed on the ground, which was one hour forty-six minutes, wet snow was falling incessantly and covered the aircraft. This snow had not been removed from the wings before the third attempted take-off. We have statements from witnesses according to which the wing surface was covered with precipitation. The Inquiry Commission is convinced that this precipitation turned into a firm layer of ice on the third take-off. On the basis of very thorough investigation and a great deal of thought, the experts discussing this question have told the Commission that this precipitation was identical with the layer of ice which was found after the accident.

Thain left the inquiry convinced that the Commission had already made up their minds, despite the scientific evidence produced by the British, and that he would be made the scapegoat. He flew home to await the Commission's written report.

Still suspended on full pay from flying duties, he passed his time as best as he could working on his poultry farm. But the long wait for the outcome of the inquiry, which would determine his future, began to put a great strain on him. All the time he knew the finger of suspicion pointed at him as the man who had caused the disaster and was responsible for the deaths of twenty-three people.

In November, with his licence due to expire, he approached Milward, the chief executive of the airline, and asked if the BEA Air Safety Committee could intervene and look at his case before the Germans issued their report. Although Milward and the Committee had great sympathy with Thain's predicament, they told him there was nothing they could do until they had read the findings of the German report. A further request from Thain for BEA, in the meantime, to find him other duties to do within the company was met with the same response.

However, there was some good news for Thain, when the

Accident Study Group, part of his union BALPA, made their own investigations into the accident and sent their findings to Lord Balfour, chairman of the BEA Air Safety Committee. Part of the report read:

> The over-running of the runway was due to some extraneous force which resulted in a deceleration of the aircraft, thereby preventing it from reaching its flying speed. The most probable cause of this is considered to be the presence of slush on the runway.

Thain was heartened by this and took solace that at least his union and some of his colleagues fully supported him. But it was not to last.

The end of the year came to a close and Thain's licence duly expired. He was now at his lowest ebb and he thought that if the situation continued for much longer he would go out of his mind. Then in February, one year after the accident, he was informed that a copy of the translated report would be in his hands on 9 March and the BEA Air Safety Committee would meet and issue its own findings on 11 March.

Thain, who knew from his own observations at the inquiry that the Germans had made up their minds as to the cause within hours of the crash, was not surprised in the least by the report's contents. The 'decisive cause', the report said, but not the 'sole cause', was a layer of ice on the wings and flying surfaces that prevented the aircraft attaining sufficient flying speed in the length of the runway available for take-off, and that slush on the runway had no appreciable effect in retarding the acceleration. The report also pointed out other factors that might have contributed to the accident. One possibility was that there was some confusion on the flight deck and the pilots acted in opposition during the final phase of the take-off run, with Rayment braking while Thain kept the throttles fully forward, and this accounted for the deceleration observed by Thain.

Things now began to move swiftly. Two days later, on the morning of 11 March, the BEA Air Safety Committee convened to consider the report and lost no time in issuing the following statement:

> The accident was due to the aircraft failing to reach the required speed to enable it to become airborne in the conditions prevailing.
>
> The German Commission of Inquiry had attributed this to icing of the wings, which had been described in their report as 'The decisive cause'.
>
> The committee feels unable to accept this evaluation of the importance of icing, but accepts that it was certainly a significant factor. Slush on the runway may have been another significant factor, and there may also have been other contributory causes.
>
> The committee feels it is not possible to evaluate the exact degree of importance attributable to these two factors, either singly or in combination.
>
> The committee notes that at the time of the accident Captain Thain, designated the Captain of the aircraft, was not occupying the left-hand seat, thereby contravening Flying Staff Instructions.
>
> The committee notes that the aircraft was not de-iced at Munich.

These findings did not bode well for Thain. Now the question remained as to what was going to happen to his licence? In the rush to judgment he didn't have to wait long. On the evening of 12 March, just three days after he had received his copy of the report, Thain was at home discussing various points of the findings with his wife, Ruby, when there was a knock on the door. There framed in the doorway was a dispatch-rider who handed him an official letter from the Ministry of Transport and Civil Aviation. Thain tore open the envelope and withdrew the contents. What he read stunned him.

> Sir,
> I am directed by the Minister to refer to the report of the

German Commission of Inquiry into the accident to Elizabethan aircraft G-ALZU at Munich on 6 February 1958 of which you already have a copy. The report deals with various factors that may have contributed to the disaster but states categorically that 'the accident would not have occurred if the aircraft had not been iced up'.

Article 17(6) of the Air Navigation Order, 1954, requires that before an aircraft flies or attempts to fly the person-in-command should satisfy himself that the wings and the control surfaces are free from ice and hoar frost. It is evident from the Report that the conditions prevailing at Munich during the latter part of the time that G-ALZU was on the ground were such as to lead to the formation of ice on the aircraft; and the Commission reached the conclusion that the wings were in fact iced up at the time of the final attempt to take-off. The Minister has, in these circumstances, been obliged to conclude that you failed in your duty as the person-in-command of the aircraft to ensure that the wings were free from ice. In view of this he has in mind in the event of your applying for the renewal of your Airline Transport Pilot's Licence to exercise his powers under Article 31 of the Air Navigation Order, 1954, to withhold such renewal for a suitable period. Before taking a final decision, however, the Minister will consider any representations you may wish to make.

The following day the German report was made public and the media were free to report that the deaths of twenty-three people in the Munich air disaster rested squarely on the shoulders of Captain James Thain. The Ministry of Aviation commented: 'We are satisfied that the German Commission examined all the evidence very thoroughly, and that due consideration was given to all the possibilities.'

Thain, although crushed by the findings and the threat of the suspension of his licence, was unwilling to accept the verdict. He vowed to fight on. In fact for him it was just the beginning of a long and hard battle to clear his name that would totally occupy him for the next decade.

Chapter 13
Captain Thain's Ordeal

Thain wasted no time and spared no efforts in his pursuit of further evidence that would force the Germans to reopen the inquiry and clear his name. Along the way he opened a Pandora's Box of lies, omissions and the deliberate suppression of evidence. His main bone of contention with the German report was the section that stated that the ice found on the wing by Reichel at 10 p.m. could not have formed after the crash, and must have been present during the attempted take-off. The Commission's argument was that no ice was found on the wing area behind the engines — if the ice formed after the accident, then ice would surely have formed there as well. It was a problem that occupied most of Thain's time and he discussed it often with his wife.

In the end it was Ruby Thain, a graduate chemist, who came up with the solution that had so far confounded everybody. She knew that the freezing point of water could be lowered if certain substances were dissolved in it. What, she thought, could have been mixed in the snow to prevent icing in these areas? She hit upon the possibility that the powder discharge from the fire extinguishers aimed at the fires in the engine nacelle areas could have something to do with it. What properties in this powder could prevent the formation of ice?

From her research she discovered that the main ingredient of the powder used in fire extinguishers was sodium bicarbonate — common baking powder. To test her theory, she crept out of the house in her dressing gown one frosty night with the temperature well below zero and sprinkled some baking powder on their car roof and watched as the powder reacted and the layer of ice melted. She then went to the trouble of obtaining a sample of the exact powder used in the extinguishers from the manufacturers. She dissolved the powder in water and after experimentation discovered that a concentrated solution would remain liquid at minus 4.8 degrees centigrade, much lower than the temperatures recorded at Munich on the night of the accident. The conclusion was clear: the fire extinguisher discharge directed at the fires in the region of the engine nacelles covered these areas with an effective anti-freeze. Subsequent snow falling on the powder would melt and remain in a liquid state and largely accounted for the absence of ice in these areas. It could also explain how the ice observed by Reichel six hours after the crash had formed.

Meanwhile Thain, pursuing his slush theory, gathered evidence on the condition of the runway on the day of the crash. He found that the plans of the Munich runway showed that it had been constructed with a camber, giving a difference of 12 inches between the centre line and the runway's edge. With the continuous movement of aircraft landing and taking off on the day of the accident, ridges of snow and slush were formed along the edges, causing a damming effect, with the runway retaining a depth in some places of up to 6 inches of water. Thain knew that this depth of water and slush far exceeded that of 5 centimetres, described in the German report as safe.

Thain, continuing his efforts to gather more evidence, came across an incident that occurred in the winter of 1948–49 — nine years before Munich — to a Canadair North Star airliner operated by Trans Canada Airlines. The pilot was attempting to take off from Vancouver on a surface heavily contaminated with a layer of wet slush. Charging down the runway the pilot found he could not accelerate beyond 103 mph and found it impossible to lift the nosewheel free of the runway. In many ways this incident mirrors that of Rayment's final attempt to take off from Munich, apart from the fact that the North Star, with no obstructions in its path, managed to safely come to a halt after overshooting the runway.

The Canadians carried out a full investigation into the incident and discovered that when an aircraft ploughs through a layer of slush the acceleration is severely retarded and a greater distance is required to attain flying speed. In extreme conditions the slush resistance can be so much that it nullifies the thrust available, preventing further acceleration. Also in certain circumstances the resistance of the slush on the main wheels can force the nosewheel down so hard that the pilot is unable, no matter how much force he exerts on the controls, to lift it free from the runway. The Canadians, in their published report, suggested that take-offs should not be attempted if the slush is more than 2 inches in depth, and that 'if the nosewheel cannot be lifted, it should be regarded as an immediate warning of trouble'.

This is exactly the same warning included in the KLM flight manuals that came to light soon after the Munich accident. The chief engineer of Trans Canada Airlines, on receiving the report of the dangers of slush after the North Star incident, quite rightly, in the interests of air safety, sent copies to all the world's major airlines — including BEA. But just as they had done before with the reports submitted from their own crews, they filed it away and did nothing, leaving their pilots to continue to sweat it out as they charged down slush-covered runways, struggling to lift their nosewheels. If BEA had acted upon this vital information seven years earlier and issued guidelines to its flight crews, then Rayment would certainly have appreciated the significance of his difficulty in raising the nosewheel from the runway at Munich, and immediately abandoned the take-off and probably avoided the fatal crash.

Back in Germany, Bill Black, the BEA engineer working on Thain's behalf, had tracked down two local engineers who worked for Pan American Airlines at Munich Airport and had been involved in the rescue operations. After some coaxing they agreed to write brief accounts of what happened at the crash scene. These statements were sent by Black to London, and after translation added to Thain's ever-growing file of new evidence.

The two men were Otto Seffer and his son Karl-Heinz; both had been involved in the rescue of Captain Rayment from the shattered cockpit. The older Seffer was somewhat vague about the state of the wings during this operation. But his son, Karl-Heinz — who actually helped prepare Zulu Uniform for departure that afternoon — had a very interesting story to tell.

After helping two injured people who were trapped by wreckage on the outside of the aircraft, he entered the fuselage and climbed into the battered cockpit to assist those who were trying to free the pilot. He said:

> My attempt to help him from the inside failed. So I then climbed up on to the fuselage at about the height of the cockpit window on the right side, and from there I helped free Captain Rayment and pulled him out of the cockpit. After this had been done successfully I climbed down from the upper side of the fuselage between the engine and the fuselage over the right wing, getting down on the rear side of the wing. In doing this I noticed no ice deposit on the fuselage or on this part of the wing. I was wearing wellington boots. I take it as a fact that no ice was present because otherwise I would most likely have slipped.

The portion of the wing, inboard of the engine, where Karl-Heinz Seffer had scrambled over was one of the very places where Reichel had discovered a layer of ice six hours after the crash. Unless Karl-Heinz was a liar, his testimony proved beyond doubt that the ice found on the wing must have formed in the hours after the accident.

Under Annex 13 of the ICAO Convention, Kelly, as the British accredited representative at the inquiry, was entitled and should have been given access to all the documents pertinent to the inquiry before it commenced, and clearly he had not. On 2 July 1959 Thain, determined to obtain copies of all the witness statements, asked Kelly to intervene. Two months later, after a great deal of prevarication, the Germans complied and Kelly in turn presented Thain with a somewhat incomplete set of documents from the Germans.

Incomplete as they were, Thain found two witness statements which were explosive reading. The witnesses were Lass and Gentzsch, the air traffic control officers on duty in the tower on the day of the accident — the very men that had communicated with Zulu Uniform during the take-off run. Part of Lass's account, written two days after the accident while the events were still fresh in his mind, states:

> The aircraft gradually built up speed, the nosewheel leaving the ground approximately halfway along the runway, but the aircraft did not become airborne within a period which could be considered normal. I then observed that the pilot pressed the nose of the aircraft down again, until the nosewheel touched the ground, as if he wanted to gain extra play in order to pull the aircraft off the runway. The nose [wheel] did in fact leave the ground once again before the end of the runway, but I could not make out with the naked eye whether the aircraft actually became airborne.

Here were two professional air traffic control officers, who were expert witnesses, yet their statements were withheld and they had not even been invited by Reichel to give evidence to the Commission. This latest discovery raised grave doubts about the whole conduct of the original inquiry. Who, Thain wanted to know, had deliberately buried these reports, and why? Lass's statement is crucial in that it describes exactly the behaviour of the aircraft that would be expected according to Thain's slush theory.

With the evidence he had already amassed, Thain sent off a series of submissions to Stimpel with a request to reopen the inquiry, commenting that this new evidence 'completely contradicts the theories advanced by the Commission as to the cause of the accident'. Thain waited in anticipation for the outcome. But it would take another five months before the Commission finally got together to consider Thain's request. Finally, on 14 March 1960, the Germans published a document entitled 'Decision'; announcing their conclusions, it said 'that the facts, evidence and other points to which the attention of the

Commission was drawn, do not justify the reopening of the proceedings'. In an accompanying document they gave their reasons for rejecting Thain's evidence.

They dismissed the statements of Otto and Karl-Heinz Seffer because none of the men had, in the Commission's words, 'paid any special attention to the wings outboard of the engines'. The fact that Karl-Heinz was adamant he found no ice on the wing inboard of the engine, where Reichel claimed to have found some six hours later, was conveniently disregarded.

Ruby Thain's research into the fire extinguisher powder was also similarly passed over. The Commission commented: 'All available reports regarding the activities of the fire fighting services show that those parts of the wreckage lay outside the main centres of fire. There is no indication that on the upper surfaces of the wings — particularly in the region of the engines — any extinguishing measures were necessary or extinguishing agents deposited, therefore Captain Thain's explanation of the absence of ice in the region of the engines cannot be regarded as correct.'

Commenting on the evidence of the condition of the runway, the Commission was equally dismissive. It was, they said, 'out of the question that any quantities of water or melted snow worth mentioning should have collected anywhere'. They totally ignored the evidence of other pilots who landed at Munich that day who reported large areas of slush and standing water on the last third of the runway, preferring to rely exclusively on the evidence of Bartz, who made only a cursory check of the mile-long runway, amazingly in just four minutes.

The only evidence left for the Commission to demolish was that of the air traffic controllers, Lass and Gentzsch. This was a more knotty problem, but as resourceful as ever they found a way around it. In the document they made a startling admission — they could do nothing else now it had been exposed — that they had had their statements right from the outset and their evidence was given due consideration when they made their findings. They could give no explanation, or offer any comment, as to why they were not called to the inquiry and be submitted to questioning. They also added that the controllers observed the critical phase of the take-off 'only from a considerable distance'. But in fact they were closer than the airport trainees, who were invited to the inquiry and whose testimony was accepted without question.

So that was it; with careful distortion of the new evidence presented by Thain, the Commission retreated behind their original judgement and under no circumstances would they consider reopening the inquiry. Thain was naturally angered by the verdict and immediately fired off a press statement:

> The refusal of the German Commission to reopen the Munich inquiry is to be regretted. Having regard to the fact that part of the evidence which was submitted clearly indicated that there was no ice on the wing immediately after the accident, and also that the two reports of the Air Traffic Controllers who saw the actual take-off were not disclosed at the inquiry, it is difficult to understand how the German authorities can justify such an arbitrary decision.

The authority of the Ministry of Aviation to revoke Thain's licence without conducting its own investigation into the matter was called into question by his union BALPA and questions were even asked in the House of Commons about his shoddy treatment by the Ministry. It was therefore decided, before any official decision was made, that an independent hearing would be convened to review whether Thain's duties as captain had been properly performed on the day of the accident. The purpose of the hearing was to enable Thain to present his case and put all the known facts in front of the reviewing body. It was not convened to assess the cause of the accident, and in no sense was it a Court of Inquiry, but the evidence, old and new, would feature prominently.

The hearing, chaired by Mr Fay, opened on 4 April 1960, in public, at 10 Carlton House Terrace in London. Thain, from the outset, wanted to present his own case but his union, BALPA, convinced him that he should have professional legal support and instructed James Comyn to represent him. Although Comyn was fully briefed, he struggled at times with some of the technical intricacies of aerodynamics and once remarked that the complexities of the subject were at times beyond him.

Under the terms of the hearing Mr Comyn was there, in the main, to prove that Thain had carried out his duties properly and taken sufficient steps to ensure that the wings of his aircraft were free from snow and ice before departure. He told the chairman:

It is not, of course, necessary for me in this representation to your body to suggest that slush was undoubtedly the cause. It is sufficient for me to show that icing was not present, and was not the cause, and to say that slush is a probable likely cause which fits in with the known facts in evidence.

The first day of the hearing was totally occupied with the exposition of Thain's case as Comyn waded through everything from boost surging to ice accretion, as well as all the witness statements. On the second day Mr Comyn called Captain Wright, a BEA pilot, to give evidence on behalf of Thain.

Just before Zulu Uniform taxied onto the runway to make its third attempt to take off, Captain Wright had landed his Viscount at Munich for refuelling on his way from Athens to London. He taxied to the far end of the runway before turning onto the perimeter track to make his way to the apron. A week later he submitted a report to the BEA Air Safety Branch on the condition of the runway because he thought it might have some bearing on the accident to Zulu Uniform. The German Commission briefly referred to the incident in their report but Captain Wright had not been invited to give his evidence first-hand at the inquiry.

Mr Comyn asked Captain Wright to describe to the hearing the depth of slush he observed on the runway when he landed at Munich shortly before three o'clock on the day of the accident.

In places, particularly the north-east end, the first two thirds approximately of the runway, I estimated it to be, by the ruts cut by the aircraft, an inch to an inch and a half. The latter part of the runway was more slush than snow — slush and snow, with patches of water. On each side of the runway there were banks of snow where the runway had, at some time previously, been cleared, but they were not very high, I would say about seven or eight inches high. But the actual runway itself towards that end was covered in slush and pools of water.

Another thing that came to light during the hearing, and which bolstered Thain's slush theory, was the information that in December 1958, ten months after Munich, BEA had issued advisory instructions to their pilots regarding taking off in Viscounts in slush and snow — by this time the Elizabethans had been withdrawn from service. Part of the instruction stated:

In most cases lack of acceleration will be apparent during the take-off run if the snow or slush is causing serious retardation. If the aircraft starts a pitching movement which is difficult to control with the elevators, or if the nosewheel is difficult to lift, these are danger warnings and take-offs should be discontinued.

In issuing these guidelines it seemed that BEA had now caught up and come into line with the policy of KLM and other airlines regarding contaminated runways, and in so doing indirectly supported Thain's view on the cause of the accident.

After four days of deliberation and the reviewing of all the evidence, old and new, Mr Fay brought the proceedings to a close. Thain came away with little cause to hope that the outcome would favour him. In July, while Thain waited for the publication of the Fay report, there came some astonishing news. Manchester United's long-drawn-out court case against BEA alleging negligence, due to be heard in the High Court in two weeks' time, was suddenly dropped without explanation. United, who were initially suing the airline for £250,000, agreed without protest to an out of court settlement of £35,000. It seems that one of the aviation experts brought in by the club to prepare evidence on which much of the case would rest came to the conclusion that icing on the wings was at the most of marginal significance, and then only when conditions were already very critical owing to slush.

Finally, in September, copies of the Fay report were sent to all the interested parties, including Thain. Its conclusion stated that

Captain Thain had not conducted his duties properly in assessing whether the wings were clear of snow and ice. The verdict was another crushing blow for Thain, but in itself should not affect his return to flying.

The Fay report was not made public until 12 October, over two and a half years since the disaster, during which time Thain had been grounded by BEA. The Ministry of Aviation conceded that his time away from flying far exceeded any period of suspension that might have been imposed on him by the Ministry and duly offered him the return of his licence. After his long spell away from flying he would, of course, have to undergo various tests and examinations and demonstrate evidence of his piloting ability. Thain knew that this would not present him with any difficulties.

On hearing the Ministry's announcement of the return of his licence Thain was overjoyed and naively told a journalist, 'The next move is to see my BEA bosses. I expect they will be sending for me in a day or so.' But it wasn't going to be as simple or clear-cut as that. In his enthusiasm to return to flying Thain had totally misread the situation. The ongoing dark conspiracy against him was soon to take a dramatic turn.

Since the accident Thain was considered by the upper echelons of BEA *persona non grata*. He was, as far as they were concerned, a commercial liability; they certainly didn't want their passengers to discover that the pilot up front on the flight deck of one of their aircraft was the man responsible for the deaths of twenty-three people at Munich. In their view Thain had to go, and they acted quickly and decisively.

On the day following the publication of the Fay report, Thain received a letter from Captain James, the BEA Flight Operations Director:

Now that the Report of the Fay Commission has been published, I am writing to you regarding the disciplinary hearing which was held in my office on 27 and 29 April 1959. You will remember that the findings of this hearing were held back, firstly pending the publication of the German Report, and subsequently pending the Fay Report.

At the disciplinary hearing the charges against you were:

(a) You did not occupy the left-hand seat, thereby contravening Flying Staff Instruction 72/56.

(b) You failed to ensure that the lift surfaces of your aircraft were clear of ice and snow immediately before the final attempted take-off and thereby unnecessarily endangered the safety of your aircraft.

In view of the serious nature of these charges which my enquiry found to be proved against you I have to advise you that your service with BEA will be terminated in accordance with your Pilot's Contract. Will you please accept this letter as three months' formal notice to terminate your contract, to take effect from 1 November 1960.

On receipt of this letter a furious Thain immediately lodged an appeal, not with BEA, but with the National Joint Council for Civil Air Transport, where he felt he would get a more sympathetic hearing. In it he cited that his union, BALPA, did not accept the German Commission's evidence for ice on the wings, and that he had correctly exercised his judgement in not having the aircraft de-iced before departure.

On the second point, his infringement of the BEA seating rule was not, in itself, serious enough to warrant his sacking. Thain pointed out that he himself had evidence of at least four instances where BEA commanders had exchanged seats and no action had been taken against them. In the end the NJC found no grounds to uphold Thain's appeal and he officially left BEA on 7 February 1961 — three years and one day after the disaster. It was his fortieth birthday.

BEA's sacking of Thain while his licence had lapsed had been savage to say the least and effectively prevented him from following his career. He now had no job and no licence, and with no licence he didn't stand a cat in hell's chance of getting employment with another airline, especially with the shadow of Munich hanging over him.

For the majority of people this should have spelled the end of the whole Munich debacle, but they didn't take into account the single-mindedness, and at times bloody-mindedness, of Jim Thain. He knew beyond doubt, after all he had been through, that the German officials had not only concocted a case against him, but in so doing dealt a grievous blow to civil aviation safety by not investigating the hazards of slush. They had also blackened his name with the stigma of Munich and effectively denied him his career. For him nothing short of a complete overturning of the German Commission's verdict would do. He vowed to fight on and all his time and finances would be spent in pursuing that goal to the bitter end.

From 1961 onwards the course of events began to turn. New evidence about slush and its inherent dangers began to surface. The Ministry of Aviation had now started to issue circulars to airlines on the operational measures for dealing with take-offs from slush-covered runways and advised that 'the theoretical limiting depth is of the order of one inch, and may be as low as half an inch'.

Then the Americans began to take the subject of slush very seriously after an incident at Idlewild Airport in 1959 when a fully laden Boeing 707, taking off on a slush-covered runway, just managed to clear the perimeter fence by an estimated 5 feet! The US Federal Aviation Agency were called on to investigate the incident and in the spring of 1961 embarked on a series of exhaustive slush trials that amassed a great deal of technical data, resulting in a 176-page report. In June 1962, in light of these developments, BALPA and the International Federation of Airline Pilots' Associations drew the attention of the Germans to the report and requested a reopening of the Munich inquiry. The Germans predictably steadfastly refused, pointing out that the Commission had thoroughly investigated the matter of ice and slush in 1958, and that 'no question now remains to be answered'.

By the latter end of 1963, the Royal Aircraft Establishment (RAE), Farnborough, began a long-delayed series of slush trials on a number of aircraft including an Elizabethan on loan from Dan Air. The trials were conducted in a similar manner to those previously undertaken in the United States. The Elizabethan used in these tests was configured to simulate as far as possible that of Zulu

Uniform on the day of the accident. The aircraft was propelled some fifty times through water-filled troughs and with the use of high-speed cameras and instrumentation the scientists at the RAE were able to calculate the amount of drag produced. The tests revealed that with a depth of as little as half a centimetre of slush, the Elizabethan required fifty per cent more runway for take-off than when dry. The results, published in April 1964, clearly showed that all the suspicions Thain had had from the very beginning regarding the effects of slush on the Munich runway were confirmed, and as far as he was concerned dismantled once and for all the credibility of the German report.

Armed with the report on the RAE slush trials, Thain, eager to progress his case, pressed the Minister of Aviation, Julian Amery, to approach the Germans again. The minister, sympathising with Thain's plight, acquiesced and sent a copy of the report together with a robustly worded letter to the Commission, asking them to examine the new evidence and consider reopening the inquiry. The West German Federal Minister of Transport, Dr Hans-Christoph Seebohm, responded, suggesting that before a new inquiry could be considered the British and German parties should meet to assess whether the evidence was sufficient to justify a reopening. After a long delay the parties eventually got together, and after various discussions the Federal Minister surprisingly announced in November 1964 that the new evidence was of significance and ordered the inquiry to be reopened. But it would be another year before the proceedings got underway.

On 18 November 1965, now nearly eight years after the accident, the inquiry reopened in Munich. The new-look Commission was chaired by Dr Hermann Rupprecht, assisted by two new assessors. Not surprisingly, and to Thain's dismay, one of the Commission members was his old adversary Reichel, who had been brought out of retirement to attend at the expressed wish of Count zu Castell, the director of Munich Airport. It was no secret that Reichel had let it be known months before the proceedings started that in his opinion 'the next investigation would only confirm the findings of the first'.

On the British side Kelly attended once again in his capacity as the accredited representative. With him were Illingworth and Maltby, the scientists from the RAE who had conducted the slush trials on the Elizabethan. Also on the British team was J. B. Veal, the head of the Accident Investigation Branch. Thain didn't want him there because of his apparent cool indifference to Thain's cause and even went so far as to secure an interview with the then Minister of Aviation, Roy Jenkins, to express his dissatisfaction at his inclusion in the party. For their part BEA sent Captain Poole and J. Kenward, and BALPA was represented by Captain Merrifield and Captain Wright.

Thain flew out to Munich a few days before the inquiry opened and settled himself in the Hotel Bayerischer Hof, where one morning he was approached by a local reporter. He told Thain that his editor would like to have a word with him about a new witness that had come forward who claimed to have taken part in the rescue and had new evidence about the condition of the wing. Thain immediately sensed that this witness was of significance and hastily arranged a meeting with him in the editor's office.

The new witness was Kurt Reschke, who was at the time of the accident employed as an ambulance driver with the Bavarian Red Cross, based at the Rechts der Isar Hospital. When news of the crash came in, he and a Dr Huber from the hospital rushed to the disaster scene. On arrival he found the right wing tip was tilted close to the ground, and it was from this point that he saw the rescuers running the entire length of the wing in their efforts to reach Rayment in the cockpit. They were wearing ordinary footwear and experienced no difficulty maintaining their footing. As Dr Huber prepared to join them, Reschke assisted him onto the wing. He told Thain:

It was somewhere between the engine and the wing tip. As he made his way up the wing he was moving absolutely freely in his ordinary shoes. When he reached the fuselage I stopped below and asked him whether I could be of any more help. In doing so I touched the back edge of the wing, considerably higher than my chest, about the level of my neck. The metal of the wing didn't feel especially cold, but moist, probably owing to the falling snow which melted on the surface. Under no circumstances did I feel ice or frozen snow.

On the back of an envelope Thain sketched out a plan of the Elizabethan and asked Reschke to mark the point where he had touched the wing. The position was the very same place where Karl-Heinz Seffer climbed down and one of the places where Reichel claimed he found the layer of ice six hours later. Reschke imparted to Thain that he would be happy to repeat his statement under oath at the inquiry if necessary. Thain came away from the meeting elated; here again was yet another witness who proved beyond doubt that there was no ice on the wings immediately after the crash. He hoped to introduce Reschke as a witness on his behalf.

Thain confidently looked forward to the inquiry, convinced that for the first time in the seven years since the accident justice would now prevail. But if he thought his long nightmare was coming to an end he was in for a shock. The Germans, it seemed, had their own agenda of how the inquiry would be conducted. Although they were prepared to listen to the new evidence presented by the British regarding the slush trials, they were adamant that no new witnesses would be called.

On the first day of the hearing Rupprecht, in his opening address, ominously remarked:

The Commission has reached the conclusion that the findings as to the circumstances of the accident, and the external conditions on the day of the accident which were reached with exemplary thoroughness at the time, can and must be taken as the basis for this inquiry.

With those words Thain's heart fell and he knew that his journey to Munich had been a complete waste of time and the outcome of the inquiry, before it had even started, was a foregone conclusion. The two air traffic controllers who had been effectively kept under the carpet at the first inquiry would now not be heard. Neither would the crucial testimony of Karl-Heinz Seffer and Kurt

Reschke, whose evidence directly contradicted that of the German Commission. Thain knew that without the introduction of these new witnesses all his hopes of the truth coming out and his name being cleared were dashed. From that point on the proceedings were no more that a calculated stage-managed farce of the highest order by the Germans. There were even times when Rupprecht faded down the microphones of those witnesses whose views he didn't want to hear, and on one occasion switched off Thain's microphone while he was still speaking. With these tactics the Commission kept a firm grip on the proceedings.

After two, in Thain's view, pointless and frustrating days the inquiry came to a close, with Rupprecht promising that all the evidence put before him would be carefully evaluated and considered. With that Thain and his party returned home to await the published report. Thain was in no doubt what the outcome would be; nevertheless he was interested to see how the Commission, this time, would manipulate the evidence to fit their 'ice on the wings' assertion.

A draft copy of the German report eventually landed on the desk of the Ministry of Aviation in London for the British to consider and make their comments before translation and publication in the UK. There were no surprises in the contents. In summary it said: 'Icing was still to be regarded as an essential cause of the accident', but went so far as to concede that 'slush, however, could be regarded as a further cause'. They also added that 'the command situation on board G-ALZU was not entirely clear-cut and may also have had an unfavourable influence on the take-off process'. Dealing with the written statement of Kurt Reschke — he had not been allowed to attend the inquiry personally — the Commission made the most implausible statement so far: 'Reschke's repeated comment to the effect that the rescuers did not slip on the wing points precisely to the presence of a deposit of rough ice which prevented their slipping.'

The British baulked at the distorted facts in the report, which now resembled little more than a work of fiction, and implored the Germans to amend their findings, but they would not be swayed. In April 1966, with the Germans unwilling to budge, the British, to their credit, issued their own conclusions that completely rebuked that of the Rupprecht Commission. 'We conclude that there is a strong likelihood that there was no significant wing icing during the take-off . . . we conclude that the principal cause of the accident was the effect of slush on the runway.' But the Germans were resolute in their verdict and regarded the subject as closed, and with undisguised indifference went ahead and published the report in Germany in September.

Finally, in October 1967, the translated German report was published in the UK. Strangely, the British included in the publication, as an appendix, the RAE slush tests memorandum — a document that directly opposed the German findings. What was to be made of this ambiguity? It seemed to be saying that the British authorities both accepts and doesn't accept the Commission findings. Was it their way of avoiding taking sides in the dispute and hoping, like the Germans, that the subject was now closed and would finally go away? Thain, commenting on the verdict, didn't hold back his venom: 'The German report is a disgrace, probably the worst piece of accident investigation I have ever seen.'

Thain knew that the Germans had nailed their colours to the mast and under no circumstances would they change their minds. His only chance now left was to drum up support and pressure the British authorities for a new inquiry of their own. He and his supporters lost no time and sent a bulky document to every MP and newspaper editor in the country, outlining the disputed and suppressed evidence. Time passed with little progress, then just as Thain's campaign seemed to running out of steam a timely comment by Prime Minister Harold Wilson changed the whole course of events.

On 2 December Wilson was a guest at a football match at Old Trafford, and during the after-match dinner that followed the subject of the Munich disaster inevitably cropped up. Wilson said that, in his view 'the captain of that aircraft has been unjustly treated ever since'. The following day the newspapers picked up on his comments and renewed public interest in the long-drawn-out Munich saga. After debating Thain's case in the House of

Commons and further wrangling with the Germans, Wilson finally announced that a new British hearing would be held. It would be the most thorough investigation into the accident so far.

However, there were those civil servants in the government who tried their best to scupper attempts to hold a fresh inquiry, despite agreeing that it would clear Thain of blame; even the British ambassador in Bonn warned the government that such a move would cause a damaging diplomatic row with Germany.

The sessions opened in private on Monday 10 June 1968, again under the chairmanship of Mr Fay, at 6 Burlington Gardens, London. Thain knew in all probability that this was his last chance; if he didn't succeed here then his decade-long battle to find justice and clear his name was all but over.

The first day of the hearing got under way with the formal reading of the terms of the inquiry, which was whether, in their opinion, blame for the accident was to be imputed to Captain Thain. There then followed a long exposition outlining the circumstances of the accident and the reading of various passages from the previous reports which the tribunal would be examining. The list of the German witnesses invited to the inquiry to give evidence was far shorter than expected — of the sixteen who had been approached only six would be attending. Many of those who declined said they had nothing to add to their statements made ten years ago. It is not difficult to deduce that pressure had been put on these witnesses by the German authorities not to appear. It is also telling that Reichel chose not to travel to London to testify.

The tribunal did not sit on the Tuesday, and the following morning was spent at Gatwick Airport inspecting a Dan Air Elizabethan, identical to that involved in the Munich accident. After lunch the first of the German witnesses were called to give evidence and to be cross-examined. Most of them had little more to add to what they had already said previously. Karl-Heinz Seffer, when giving his evidence, was able to identify himself in one press photograph standing on top of the fuselage with his father, and in another walking along the starboard wing, which he claimed was free from ice and where he had no difficulty maintaining his footing. Reschke also indicated on a photograph the position where he had helped Dr Huber climb on the wing and the place where he had touched the surface. He told the inquiry how he deduced it was not below freezing point. 'You appreciate,' he explained, 'that if you touch metal with your bare hands and it is below freezing point your skin will stick to it, but this did not occur. I could slide my hands quite freely over the metal.'

The remainder of the day was occupied by the testimony of the two key witnesses which had from the very beginning shaped the case against Thain. They were Kurt Bartz, who in 1958 was the airport manager and responsible for the condition of the runway at Munich, and Count zu Castell, the airport director. After Bartz's original statement was read out to the tribunal Thain's counsel, John May QC, cross-examined him on the extraordinary speed of his inspection of the runway, the discrepancies in the number of times he claimed to have left his car to measure the depth of slush and his steadfast insistence that the runway was perfectly flat, despite evidence to the contrary. Bartz refused to be drawn by May's questions and would not comment beyond his original statement. Similarly Castell, in his concern for the reputation of Munich Airport and himself, would not comment further than the confines of his first statement. As far as he was concerned the fact that the West German Chancellor landed safely shortly after the crash clearly demonstrated that there was nothing amiss with *his* runway.

Day Four of the proceedings started on a sensational note when the first witness of the day brought to light for the first time the deliberate tampering of evidence by the Germans. The witness was Hans-Georg Brehme, who at the time of the accident was a lieutenant in the army. After the accident he made a written statement to the investigators but had never been interviewed, nor was he called upon to appear before the Commission, but part of his statement was briefly alluded to in one of the German reports. As his statement was being read out Brehme interrupted the proceedings, saying that what was being quoted bore no resemblance to the statement he had made. Fortunately he had brought with him a copy of the original, which he read out to the tribunal. It turned out that the passage quoted in the German report came from Brehme's *altered* statement. Speculation was rife amongst those assembled as to who could have been the author of the bogus document. If anyone had bothered to ask Thain he would have told them.

When Brehme's evidence was completed the tribunal adjourned to watch a series of films. The first was some brief newsreel footage showing Reichel examining the wreckage of the Elizabethan on the night of the accident. The second was an American-made film demonstrating the hazards of slush. With that the inquiry team reassembled to hear the technical evidence regarding slush and its effects on aircraft performance. This turned out to be the crux of the inquiry and continued for several days.

Mr Maltby and Mr Illingworth, experts from the RAE, in their evidence gave the view that it was necessary to take a large number of measurements to accurately assess the depth of slush on a runway. Maltby said, 'On one occasion I employed something like twenty people to measure the depth of slush on a runway 10,000 feet long and 300 feet wide.' This evidence completely discredited the reliability of Bartz, who was convinced that there was an even deposit over the entire Munich runway, so level that the only difference between the 5 or 7 millimetres he observed was caused by the runway's slight camber. It is only rarely that snow falls so regularly as to produce a completely even cover. On the day of the accident the wind was blowing at 8 knots and from eleven o'clock in the morning there had been fairly severe driving snow and at least two squall fronts had passed over the airport. Moreover the runway was frequently disturbed and slush-scattered by aircraft landing and taking off. Bartz's cursory survey of the runway, making only two or three stops to measure the depth of slush, was now called into question.

Without doubt the star witness in the Fay inquiry was Reinhardt Meyer, the first person on the scene of the crash; his evidence would prove to be pivotal. It had been assumed from the very beginning that he was unable to appear at the original inquiry. Meyer was now resident in the United States, but at the time of the Fay hearing he was by chance on holiday with his family in Bremen. Members of the Commission, in their search for the truth, decided to adjourn the inquiry and travel to Germany to interview him and hear his evidence first-hand.

Meyer was an aeronautical engineer and had been a pilot since 1940, making him an expert and reliable witness. On the day of the accident he was at Munich Airport on business. What he told the Commission came as a shock. He said he was first person on the scene and wondered what had possibly caused the crash.

I was thinking about possible reasons for the accident, and I know I was considering whether aircraft icing could have been the reason. I walked over and examined the wing of the wrecked aircraft and observed that *there was nothing like frost or frozen deposit; that I know definitely. There was melting snow only.*

Meyer told his astonished listeners that he had imparted this observation directly to Reichel at the time but had heard nothing more on the matter. Asked why he hadn't given this information to the inquiry, Meyer replied, 'I was not called to give evidence and I didn't even see them.' It was incredible. But what was even more incredible was that his original written statement, handed personally to Reichel, had been tampered with and his comments on the absence of ice on the wing had been deliberately removed. Meyer's evidence completely demolished once and for all the German 'ice on the wing' theory.

Reichel's handling of Meyer's evidence was deplorable. It will be remembered on the first day of the original inquiry in 1958 he told the Commission: 'I have asked Herr Meyer to be here today. Unfortunately he cannot come,' after which Reichel read out only those parts of his statement that dealt with the aircraft wheel tracks at the end of the runway, deliberately omitting his references to the absence of ice on the wings.

It was with these underhanded measures that Reichel maintained a conspiracy for over ten years that the Munich air disaster was caused by ice on the wing, thereby imputing the blame onto Thain. This was the man who, as the chief accident investigator of the West German Federal Office of Aviation, signed the formal declaration required by German law on accepting the appointment to serve on the Commission: '*I bind myself to fulfil the duties of a member of the Federal Aviation Office impartially and justly to the best of my knowledge and conscience.*'

The Fay inquiry also solved the mystery of the photograph of Zulu Uniform taken from the airport building shortly before the final take-off attempt. This appeared to show some snow adhering to the wings and was used by Reichel as credible evidence for ice on the wings in the two German reports. It was discovered that the original print been made from a copy negative, but during the inquiry the Treasury solicitor succeeded in obtaining the original. After a series of careful enlargements were made the negative was submitted for examination and interpretation and clearly showed the wing lettering and markings on the wing. Photographic experts said that in their opinion there was no sign of snow or ice lying on the upper surfaces.

Recently released classified documents show that as preparations were being made to publish the report, Foreign Office staff worried that the report would 'cast doubt on the propriety of the original investigation' and there would be 'a risk of serious damage to our relations with the Germans'. One official wrote 'our assessment is that the Germans are likely to react very sharply indeed to the publication of evidence or findings which would impugn the integrity of their investigation'.

At a secret meeting of ministers in April 1969, the Attorney General, Sir Elwyn Jones, said that 'a report which made an attack on the German inquiry would be an unhappy outcome'. But the Foreign Office minister, Lord Chalfont, cautioned: 'we could not connive at the suppression of evidence even if it meant some damage to our relations with Bonn'.

The Fay Report was handed to the president of the Board of Trade, Anthony Crosland, on 18 March 1969 and made public on 10 June. After eleven years the Fay Commission had finally arrived at the truth, which completely reversed the German findings. It said in summary:

> We are satisfied that at, or after V1 the aircraft's nosewheel re-entered the slush, had this not happened, the aircraft must have

flown off. We are equally satisfied that the descent of the nosewheel was caused by increased drag exerted through the main wheels, in other words, by the aircraft entering a trail of deeper and/or denser slush. This increase in slush drag is in our view the prime cause of the accident. We are satisfied that thereafter the aircraft ran with six wheels in the slush until towards the end of the runway it rotated to the point where the tailwheel made contact with the ground. We can be sure that the period between V1 and rotation was one of deceleration. We cannot reach certainty as to the speed at the end of the period. Once the aircraft rotated without lifting off, the accident was inevitable. There was not enough runway left to regain sufficient speed. Our considered view, therefore, is that the cause of the accident was slush on the runway. Whether wing icing was also a cause, we cannot say. It is possible, but unlikely. **In accordance with our terms of reference we therefore report that in our opinion blame for the accident is not to be imputed to Captain Thain.**

It was the end of a terrible, long-drawn-out ordeal for Thain, who understandably felt bitter towards the German authorities, who had effectively set him up from the very beginning to take the blame. Above all he had deep contempt for one individual — Reichel, who as the chief accident investigator knew all along that ice on the wing had not caused the accident; Reinhardt Meyer, amongst others, had told him so.

Commenting on the verdict, Thain said, 'I was made a scapegoat — this whole thing has carved a big chunk out of my life. If Munich hadn't happened, I suppose it's conceivable that I would be a senior captain with BEA by now, doing the job I really loved doing.' Asked by a reporter if he would ever go back to flying, he said, 'I don't know. I'm getting a long way down the runway now.'

For Thain, it was only a partial victory. The Germans refused, and to this day still refuse, to acknowledge the Fay Commission findings. He was never reinstated by BEA, who sacked him on an irrelevant charge of contravening company flying instructions. He never held a flying licence again.

Captain James Thain is to be admired, in that he never refused to give up the fight for justice and to restore his self-respect and reputation. In doing so he pushed the aviation authorities into taking the hazards of slush seriously and undertaking the vital research that probably prevented another Munich.

Chapter 14

Fifty Years On

The public persona of Busby over the years is that of a kind fatherly figure, but after he recovered and returned to Old Trafford he showed an underlying streak of ruthlessness to some of the surviving Babes in his efforts to rebuild the club and restore it to its former glory. But it is also fair to say that if he hadn't been ruthless he would never have created the greatest football club in Europe.

He kept on the surviving players who were fit enough to play: Harry Gregg, Bobby Charlton, Bill Foulkes and Dennis Viollet. But the others — Ray Wood, Albert Scanlon and the eighteen-year-old 'Welsh Wizard' Kenny Morgans, none of whom had regained their form after they returned to Old Trafford — were soon moved on without ceremony to other clubs, leaving them with a sense of betrayal.

Albert Scanlon's bitterness towards the club began soon after he stepped off the train at London Road station following the crash. Supported by crutches, he hobbled out of the station and hailed a black cab. The sympathetic driver, who wasn't even a United supporter, told Albert the cab was his free of charge until he was fully recovered. A few weeks later he was approached in the Old Trafford car park by Les Olive, the United secretary, who told him to give up the taxi as the club was not prepared to pay the fares. He had wrongly assumed that United were footing the bill. An angry Scanlon put him right in no uncertain terms, telling him it was none their business.

By the middle of the following season his form became patchy and Busby transferred him to Newcastle United for £17,000. He told Albert not to worry, that financially he would take care of things. But it turned out to be an empty promise. Five years later he saw Busby outside Old Trafford, 'and he didn't want to know me'. After spells with Lincoln and Mansfield he retired from the game at thirty and struggled to earn a living with a succession of low-paid jobs.

Kenny Morgans also lost out after Munich. Just before the crash he was going through a terrific run of form that saw him edge Johnny Berry out of the side and his future looked long and bright. After his release from hospital he made a handful of League outings and was picked to play in the FA Cup final against Bolton, but on the morning of the game Busby dropped him in favour of Dennis Viollet. It was a decision that broke his heart. After that, according to Harry Gregg, he seemed to lose a couple of yards of pace and was transferred to his home town club, Swansea. Like Scanlon, Busby promised him he would be looked after, but in reality it came to nothing. After a spell with Newport County he retired at the age of thirty, having lost all interest in football.

Johnny Berry, who suffered a fractured skull, broken pelvis and broken jaw that led to the removal of all his teeth, was extremely lucky to survive; like Busby he was given the last rites by a German priest. He wanted nothing more than to return to Old Trafford and resurrect his playing career. But it soon became clear that he would never play professional football again. There was little compassion from United for his predicament and within a year he and his wife with their eight-year-old son Neil were unceremoniously asked to vacate their club house to make way for new boy Shay Brennan. His employment cards, officially informing him of his sacking, dropped on the doormat shortly after. His wife Hilda never forgave United for their lack of compassion and the way they treated him. She was so embittered that when Johnny passed away in 1994, Harry Gregg had to ask her if it would be all right to send a wreath on behalf of the Manchester United Old Boys' Association.

Harry Gregg's best friend and teammate, Jackie Blanchflower, survived the crash with fearful injuries: smashed pelvis, serious kidney damage and almost the loss of his right arm. As soon as it became obvious that he would never play again he was, like Johnny Berry, kicked out of his club house, despite the fact that his wife was pregnant with their first child. 'It was made pretty clear we had to leave,' said his wife Jean. 'United were very cold, very harsh, after the crash.'

By January 1959, Jackie found himself on the dole and looking for a place to live. To add insult to injury, the United director (soon to become chairman) Louis Edwards offered him a labouring job in his meat packaging factory, loading pies on to lorries — he declined the offer. Years later he went back to Old Trafford to try to get tickets for a match and was turned away. After that he never returned for fear of being snubbed.

Before the disaster he was looking forward to playing alongside his friend and teammate Harry Gregg for Northern Ireland in the 1958 World Cup finals, but sadly it all came to an abrupt end in just one minute at Munich.

I never got over it. It was around eight or nine months after the crash when they told me I couldn't play again. I went to see a specialist in London who told me to pack it in. It was shattering — I really can't describe it any better. My kidneys were what they were concerned about most and they felt I could damage them again if I played. I couldn't believe them at the time, but they were right.

I've never got it right in my mind. You go through difficult phases. You look for someone to blame which is the first one, and then you get bitter. That eventually goes away and you're left with just cynicism. I can't say how it was for the others, but that's how it was for me.

I didn't get any counselling and ironically, when I was fifty-four and looking for a job, I applied for a job as counsellor but they told me I had no experience or university training. That just made me more sceptical than ever.

I'd not made any plans and then there I was left on my own in the big ugly world. I'd been cocooned playing football and all of a sudden it was gone. I bought a newspaper shop, worked for a bookmaker, moved into a pub — they all lasted around six or seven years. Then I went back to school and became a finance manager, and I've finished up as an after-dinner speaker.

For forty years none of the survivors or relatives of the victims publicly challenged the official story of Munich, feeling that to do so would be disloyal to those who died. This conspiracy of silence over what they saw as the club's failure to look after them began to be breached in the summer of 1997, when the eight surviving Babes were sent a touching letter of invitation from UEFA, the European footballing governing body, to attend the European Cup final between Borussia Dortmund and Juventus in Munich, as a mark of the enormous contribution they had made to European football. 'I had tears in my eyes,' said Ray Wood when he received his invitation. 'This was recognition, after forty years, which we never had in all that time from United.'

It was Wood who used the reunion as an opportunity to hatch a plan with the others to force United to pay them some recompense after four decades of neglect. He arranged a meeting with the rest of the Babes in the Ibis Munchen Messe hotel in Munich the day before the game to discuss the matter in detail. Some of those present expressed the view that they didn't want to include Bobby Charlton in the discussions, but as Harry Gregg rightly pointed out he was one of them and had the right to be there. In the end Charlton, for his own reasons, decided against attending.

It soon became clear that Manchester United was far too big and powerful an organisation to tackle on their own and they enlisted the help of others. A committee was constituted to represent them that included John Doherty, a former Busby Babe; David Sadler, who ran the Manchester United Former Players' Association; David Meek, a sports journalist who had covered United for over thirty years with the *Manchester Evening News*; and Gordon Taylor from the Professional Footballers' Association. Together they came up with the concept of a Munich memorial match to be played at Old Trafford with the proceeds being divided between the survivors and dependants.

But first they had the task of approaching and winning over Martin Edwards, the then United chief executive. He was the only man at the club who wielded the power to sanction such a game. Early in 1998, with little progress being made, John Doherty, in an effort to get things moving, went to see Edwards at his lavish home in Cheshire to discuss the possibility of a benefit game at Old Trafford to raise funds. According to Doherty, Edwards asked him, 'But why now John, after forty years?' His answer was short and to the point: 'Because they are fucking skint!'

Martin Edwards' association with Manchester United over three decades had made him a multimillionaire, owed in the main to his father, Louis. Louis Edwards, the head of a meat packaging empire, was appointed a director at an emergency board meeting the day after Munich. With the death of Harold Hardman in 1964 — and after six years of share buying — he was elected chairman and presided over a remarkable post-Munich recovery to the pinnacle of European Cup glory in 1968.

In 1970 the United board — chaired by his father — elected his 24-year-old son, Martin, a club director. Ten years later, on his father's death, he found himself chairman and majority shareholder. Although he frequently professed that United was his greatest love, it didn't stop him trying to cash in on their success and profitability by trying to sell the club to the highest bidder. In 1984 fraudster Robert Maxwell offered a reported £10 million for the club, but his bid was rejected as being too low. Five years later Edwards attempted to sell United again, this time to the Isle of Man property developer Michael Knighton, but in the end the deal collapsed when one of his banking backers dropped out.

In 1991 Edwards floated the club on the stock exchange with a valuation of £40 million. Further share issues followed in 1994 and 1997, with Edwards accumulating £71 million from the shares he sold. By 2000 Manchester United had become the richest club in the world, reaching the magical milestone of £1 billion. Edwards stepped down as chief executive in 2000, with his deputy, Peter

Kenyon, taking his place, but he still retained his position as chairman on a massive salary with all the perks.

In the years that followed Munich, Martin Edwards, like his father before him, refused to accept that Manchester United owed the Babes and their dependants anything. The history of the club, including that of the Busby Babes era, is something he never wanted to understand. Referred to as 'That Bastard' and 'Fartin' Martin' on some unofficial United supporters' websites, he became the most reviled of the hierarchy at Old Trafford. But like him or loathe him, he presided over the most successful period in Manchester United's long history.

Edwards' humiliating fall from grace and departure from the club came in 2002, when he was questioned by police over an alleged Peeping Tom incident in a ladies' toilet at the Mottram Hall Hotel, Cheshire, where he was a frequent visitor. According to the *Daily Mirror*, Edwards was said to have looked under the door of a toilet cubicle, leaving the woman inside feeling 'very distressed'. Edwards voluntarily attended a police station to be interviewed. A Cheshire Police spokesman said, 'A 57-year-old man was cautioned at Wilmslow Police Station in respect of Section 5 of the Public Order Act'. Not long after this incident, Peter Kenyon summoned Edwards to his office and told him in no uncertain terms, in the interest of the club, to step down from his position as chairman.

This, then, was the character of the man who in 1998 was sanctioned to approve and organise the Munich testimonial. For Edwards it was a golden opportunity to redeem his tarnished reputation with the fans and show the caring side of the world's richest club. But somehow even this chance to put things right after forty years slipped through his fingers and he turned it into a shambles of the first order.

When the decision was finally made to hold the benefit game, United and the fund committee looked around for suitable opposition and a fixture date as near as possible to the Munich anniversary. Teams that were considered because of the historical link with the disaster were Red Star Belgrade and Bayern Munich, and on the strength of this the fans bought tickets. Then, out of the blue, the former United player Eric Cantona suddenly entered the equation. According to Martin Edwards it was Cantona who approached him about wishing to return to Old Trafford to play in a farewell match. Unbelievably, Edwards decided to combine the two games. Many of the relatives and the fans were outraged. Elizabeth Wood, the divorced wife of goalkeeper Ray Wood, vented her anger in the press:

> We just want the club to give us some dignity. Offer some recognition to those who died, who gave their lives for Manchester United and gave birth to a legend. What the plc is doing is immoral, leaving us as just rubbish, simple vermin. And as for Eric Cantona, it was his decision to retire. Suddenly, the game has become the Eric Cantona roadshow, while the survivors are like dancing bears at a circus.
>
> I saw those terrible scenes in the hospital after the crash. I stayed at Ray's bedside for eight weeks and I was there when Duncan Edwards died. Ray would ask me every day who was the next to have died. The airline flew us out to Munich and gave us daily expenses. Even my local priest offered financial help — but there was nothing from United.

Cantona is probably best remembered for his violent outburst at Selhurst Park in a game against Crystal Palace in January 1995 when he launched a kungfu-style attack on a Palace fan. The player claimed the fan shouted racial insults and threw a missile at him as he walked off the pitch after he had been red-carded for kicking another player. For the unsavoury incident the football authorities banned him from playing for nine months and fined him £20,000. It wasn't the first time Cantona's fiery temper had got him into trouble. In 1987 he punched his own goalkeeper at Auxerre, leaving him with a black eye. He was also suspended by Marseilles for kicking a ball into the crowd and throwing his shirt at the referee after being substituted. He retaliated by retiring from the French premier league and moving to England, joining Leeds United before being transferred to Manchester United in 1992. In May 1997, at the age of thirty, he announced his retirement from football to pursue a new career as a film actor.

With the fortieth anniversary fast approaching, the testimonial committee was looking around for a fixture date as near as possible to 6 February. But with the whole game now revolving around Cantona this date was thrown out of the window when Cantona announced that, owing to his commitment for a starring role in a film, he would be unavailable until later in the year.

The memorial match — or the Eric Cantona Show, as it was now dubbed — finally went ahead on 18 August at Old Trafford between a Manchester United XI versus a European XI with Cantona playing a half for each side. The match had some bizarre aspects, with Mick Hucknall, the lead singer from Simply Red, serenading the Frenchman with *Every Time You Say Goodbye*. The club also used the occasion to make a few presentations that had nothing at all to do with Munich. United turned out 8–4 winners with Cantona making a lap of honour. In the end the game, which was supposed to enshrine the memory of the Babes, turned out to be little more than a farce.

Within weeks of the memorial game, the testimonial committee received an invoice from Cantona's agents for £90,500 to cover his expenses. These included the charter of a private Lear jet to fly over his friends and relatives and accommodation in a five-star hotel in Cheshire. Many of the survivors and families were rightly angered that this was deducted from the fund and felt the club should have picked up his bill. Finally, after Cantona's expenses were deducted, less tax and other expenses, it left a paltry amount of £47,000 for each of the survivors or dependants — half of what Cantona received.

Harry Gregg's opinion of the memorial game was that it was just another huge publicity stunt by the club, or as he succinctly put it, 'so much PR bullshit', with the fans pushing through the turnstiles shelling out their hard-earned cash. Gregg, always a man who steadfastly stands by his principles, had no intention of attending the match, but a phone call from Jean Blanchflower quickly caused him to change his mind. She told Harry the devastating news that Jackie was terminally ill with acute liver failure. They had been best friends for over fifty years, since they played together for Northern Ireland Schoolboys. Jackie wanted to attend the match and Gregg was not going to allow him to go on his own. It was an emotional journey back to Old Trafford for both of them; it was also their final goodbye.

Any financial benefit from the memorial game came too late for Jackie — a few weeks later, on 1 September, he passed away aged sixty-five. Nor did it help his wife, Jean; over the following three years she suffered serious circulatory problems that led to the amputation of both legs and soon after died from a fatal heart attack.

Epilogue

Joe Mercer, when he was the Manchester City manager in the late sixties, remembers the day he was invited to take part in a TV chat show in London. As he waited behind the scenes to go on, the announcer said, 'Tonight's guests are Derek Nimmo, Spike Milligan, and Joe Mercer, manager of Manchester United.' 'Blimey,' said Joe to himself, 'they've given Matt the bloody sack at last!'

Unbeknownst to Joe, Matt Busby had reluctantly stepped down as team manager that day. He told a news conference at Old Trafford that the pressures of managing a top-class team were becoming too great for a man of his age and he would now take the role of general manager. He said, 'United is no longer just a football club, it is an institution. I feel the demands are beyond one human being. It's time to make way for a younger man.'

For many years Busby felt a certain amount of guilt for what happened at Munich. He thought that if he had made some sort of protest after the second attempted take-off then he could have somehow averted the disaster. He said:

Many times I have asked myself whether there was anything I could have done, or should have done, to stop that plane. We went back to the terminal and everything seemed to have been checked. It would have been as pointless for me to ask the pilot if everything was OK as if he had asked me whether I had picked the best team for Manchester United. All you can do is repose confidence in the pilots and airline. After all, no pilot would take a chance, for his life is just as much at stake as yours.

Before that terrible day, I could see ten years ahead, ten years at the top with nothing to stop us. After it, I had two choices. I could either lie down and hide, or pick myself up and accept the challenge.

It is a matter of history that Busby accepted the challenge, returned to Old Trafford and began rebuilding another great team that included some great players, who, like the Babes, became legends — Denis Law, George Best, Nobby Stiles and Brian Kidd to name a few. In 1963 United reached the FA Cup final, defeating Leicester City 3–1 to win the trophy for the third time. With the team continuing to improve, they won the First Division Championship in 1964–65 and again in 1966–67. The title victories saw them once again embark on the European Cup trail.

On a humid May evening at Wembley in 1968, Busby's long-held European dream became reality when Manchester United were crowned European Champions with a 4–1 extra time win over Benfica, becoming the first English team to lift the trophy. Busby cried that night. The dream he thought had died along with his Babes at the end of the runway at Munich ten years earlier had finally come true. He said, 'That moment when Bobby Charlton took the cup, it cleansed me. It eased the pain of the guilt of going into Europe. It was justification.'

In the aftermath of Munich, Busby was awarded the CBE, received the Freedom of the City of Manchester in 1967 and, following United's European Cup triumph, was knighted. He was also awarded the highest civil honour in the Roman Catholic Church when Pope Paul made him a Knight Commander of St Gregory the Great. On 20 January 1994 the grand old man of English football died from blood cancer at the age of eighty-four. Football fans everywhere mourned his passing.

Munich might have spelled the end of Manchester United if it was not for Jimmy Murphy battling against overwhelming odds to hold the club together. He took over the reins in Busby's absence and from the remnants of what was left at Old Trafford put together another United team. They might have lacked the sparkle of the Babes but they were still a great team and it was 'Murphy's Marvels' that was really the start of Manchester United's legendary worldwide following.

After Busby's retirement the Manchester United of the Babes era quickly evaporated to be replaced by a club where money was at its heart. Jimmy looked on with great sadness as he saw what was happening to his beloved club. On 30 September 1971, after twenty-five years of loyal service to the club, Jimmy Murphy hung up his tracksuit and retired.

During his long years with United the number of players he helped to discover and coach to greatness is remarkable: Duncan Edwards (still regarded fifty years after his death as the greatest English player ever), Dennis Viollet, David Pegg, Roger Byrne, Eddie Colman, Albert Scanlon, Liam Whelan, Mark Jones, Bobby Charlton, George Best, Nobby Stiles and Brian Kidd were just some among the many he moulded into football legends. Other established players the club brought in from outside, such as Tommy Taylor, Albert Quixall, Denis Law and Paddy Crerand, had Jimmy to thank for developing their skills even further to make them into world-class players. It was for this outstanding record that he justly deserved his title 'The Starmaker'.

His influential contribution to the success of Manchester United is largely forgotten today by the club, its management and supporters. Apart from the Jimmy Murphy Young Player of the Year Trophy, awarded at the end of each season to the best reserve player, there is nothing — a sad reflection on the man who dedicated his life totally to United. In the aftermath of Munich he was offered £20,000 — a fortune in those days — to join Juventus as their manager. It was just one of the many offers he received during his time at Old Trafford. He turned them all down to stay loyal to Manchester United and Matt Busby right to the end. Jimmy passed away in November 1989 aged seventy-nine.

Harry Gregg, the man dubbed the hero of Munich, is now retired and living back in his Ulster homeland. In time his services to football and his bravery shown at Munich were recognised with an MBE. He reluctantly accepted the honour as a tribute to those who lost their lives in the disaster. He says, 'I did not particularly want the award. I was just happy to have got out of the crash with my life. Like many of the others, I first felt a curious sense of guilt that I had survived when so many of my friends died.' He doesn't believe that heroes and cowards are preordained. 'People are faced with a particular situation and have to react in seconds. And until that happens, it's futile to speculate what the response will be.' But whatever Harry Gregg says, when he was put to the test on that snow- and slush-covered field in Munich his character was not found wanting.

One day, eighteen years after Munich, while he was manager of Crewe Alexandra, Harry Gregg was contacted by a television company offering to bring him together with Vesna Lukic, the child he pulled from the wreckage. Harry was naturally keen to meet her again after all these years, but he wanted the meeting in private and off camera. That didn't make good TV, so the reunion fell through. He then had to endure the newspaper headline 'MUNICH HERO SNUBS THE CHILD HE SAVED'. Gregg said, 'I couldn't do right for doing wrong.'

But in time he did meet Vesna and her mother Verena on a TV programme hosted by ex-Liverpool player Ian St John. It was an emotional reunion, where Gregg admits he broke down and cried for the first time since hearing the news of Duncan Edwards' death. It turned out that Gregg had saved three lives that day — he discovered that Verena had been pregnant at the time and later gave birth to a son.

Captain James Thain, his name finally cleared, continued to run his poultry farm as well as farming 30 acres of land in Berkshire. Unhappy that the Germans refused to accept the verdict of the Fay Report, he stepped up the pressure on them to reopen their inquiry, but unfortunately his campaign fizzled out. In 1975 his eleven-year struggle to find justice finally took its toll and he died prematurely of a heart attack aged just fifty-four, bringing to mind an old aviation adage: 'If the accident doesn't kill the pilot, the inquiry will'. There were twenty-three victims at Munich; Captain

James Thain became the twenty-fourth.

The last word in this story goes to Matt Busby. Returning to Old Trafford for the first time after the Munich disaster, he said:

> When I approached the ground and moved over the bridge along which our supporters had squeezed fifty abreast in their tens of thousands to shout for us, I could scarcely bear to look. I knew the ghosts of the Babes would still be there, and are there still, and they will always be there as long as those who saw them play still cross the bridge — young red ghosts on the green grass of Old Trafford.

For the rest of his life the Babes were never far from his mind. There were many times when the memory of Munich and players lost would cast a dark shadow over his face. It was at these times he would turn to a close friend and whisper in their ear: 'Sometimes I still see them play.'

Index